MILLGATE
AYLSHAM

Further details of Poppyland titles can be found at
www.poppyland.co.uk
where clicking on the 'Support and Resources' button
will lead to pages specially compiled to support this title.

Extract from the Ordnance Survey map of 1906

10.95

AYLSHAM LOCAL HISTORY SOCIETY

Millgate
Aylsham

A study by
the Local History Research Group

SECOND EDITION
edited by Tom Mollard & Geoff Gale

First published by the Aylsham Local History Society in 1993
Second edition published 2006 by Poppyland Publishing, Cromer NR27 9AN
Reprinted 2013

ISBN 0 946148 79 1 / 978 946148 79 0

Designed and typeset in 11/14 pt Bembo by Watermark, Cromer, NR27 9HL

Printed by Lightning Source UK Ltd

Contents

Lithograph showing Aylsham Bridge over the River Bure, with the Anchor Inn in the background; from a set of drawings by Francis Stone' and son depicting Norfolk bridges, published in 1830.

Preface to the Revised Edition

The original edition of *Millgate* was published in 1993 and is now no longer available. The Aylsham Local History Society has been considering whether simply to republish the book as it was, or to commission some new material and publish it as a new edition. As you will see we decided on the latter course and we hope you will enjoy this revised version of *Millgate*.

This 2006 edition includes three new chapters which illustrate some different aspects of life in Millgate and a more detailed piece of writing on the Anchor Inn. The additional work on the Anchor Inn now forms part of the chapter on Millgate public houses. We have also included a chapter by Ben Rust on the millers in the area which was first published in the Society's Journal in June 1992. It seemed appropriate to revive and include this article since milling was an important industry in Millgate. There is also a new chapter on the Belt estate, the Wickes and the other families that had owned the estate.

In the 12 years between these two editions a number of changes have taken place in Millgate; buildings have been sold, some have been altered and others demolished. The editors have therefore had to make adjustments to the original text to reflect these changes. The introduction of the new chapters necessitated some rewriting to correct any repetition between the new and the original text. The order of chapters is slightly different from that of the first edition because of this new material. However the illustrations by Peter Holman remain from the first edition, supplemented with some additional illustrations and maps. The cover has again been adapted from the map of Aylsham by Peter Holman, but this time we are able to print it in colour.

The editors are grateful to each of the contributors and to Peter Holman for his illustrations and to Felicity Cox and Roger Polhill for their help and suggestions on the contents of the book and for their assiduous proof-reading of the text. Our thanks to the Federation of Norfolk Historical and Archaeological Organisations for their grant to help with the cost of production.

G.G. T.M.

Millgate, near the Stonemason's Arms (now a private house)

Foreword to the First Edition

Soon after the Aylsham Local History Society was formed in 1984, Mr Tom Bishop of Bridge House, Millgate, offered a bundle of deeds in his possession to the Society for examination, believing that they might be of historical interest. A quick superficial survey of their contents revealed that they indeed contained much information about properties mostly, but not entirely, in Millgate, and covered a period from about 1750 onwards. At this time, no one in the membership was available to study them in detail.

However, as the membership has grown, a 'research group' has come into being, and has been meeting regularly over a period of years, gradually acquiring some skills in reading and appraising documents.

Two years ago, the corner of Aylsham we call Millgate seemed a suitable portion of the town for group study. Mr Bishop was happy to lend out his documents, and the project got under way with Christopher Barringer, Director of Extra-Mural Studies at the University of East Anglia, as tutor.

In our two years of study we have sought not only to learn what the 'Bishop Bundles' (as they have come to be called) can tell us about Millgate, but to relate that information to that obtained from other historical sources. The resulting book is an account of what we have learnt about the properties in the area, the people who owned and lived in them, their life-style and how they earned their living during this period. Millgate emerges as an area of Aylsham made distinctive by its growth round the river and the mill, yet remaining an integral part of the larger market town community.

We are grateful to Christopher Barringer for his advice and support in the carrying forward of this project.

Contributors over the two year period include the following: Anne Applin, Ray Balls, Valerie Belton, Alan Coote, Eileen Daines, Julian Eve, Gill Fletcher, Elizabeth Gale, Geoffrey Gale, Betty Gee, Peter Holman, Tom Mollard, Kay Mosse, Jane Nolan, Frank Stageman, Maureen Strong, Joan Turville-Petre and Wenda Wiles.

Jane Nolan
Chairman
Aylsham Local History Society

I

Millgate: an introduction

by Christopher Barringer

The market town of Aylsham survives, relatively untouched by the processes of industrialisation in the nineteenth century and by the worst effects of the motor car, shopping malls, and the post-modern return to stockbrokers' Tudor that is fast afflicting housing estates. The beautiful parish church stands high above the valley of the River Bure with the market place close up against its southern side. The market place is surrounded by many sixteenth, seventeenth and eighteenth century buildings, as well as some more recent ones. Hungate, Red Lion and White Hart Streets lead to the market place and also have many fine pre-nineteenth century buildings bordering them. Two miles to the west of Aylsham lies the Blickling estate which provides a boundary to Aylsham on its western side, and has also had an important influence on the evolution and character of the town.

This book is primarily concerned with Millgate, the road which links the core of Aylsham around the market place with the water mill on the Bure. Millgate does, in some ways, qualify as the nineteenth century part of the town, although the important water mill almost certainly dates from pre-Domesday times, and a cluster of buildings between the mill and the 'great bridge' includes a number of pre-nineteenth century survivals. The opening of the Bure Navigation in 1779 linked Aylsham by canal and river with Yarmouth and the Broadland river system. The development led to the rapid growth of new occupations such as wherryman and boat builder, and also increased the outlets for the malting trade in Aylsham. This, in turn, led to families such as the Spurrells and Parmeters becoming important members of the Aylsham community. By focussing on a small part of the town, it was hoped that it would be possible to follow the fortunes of some families and some of their houses within a relatively limited part of the larger community of Aylsham.

This study does not aim to look at Millgate as far back as 1624, the date of an important survey of Aylsham which was transcribed and published as *Aylsham in the Seventeenth Century* (Poppyland, 1988). However, one or two points about the medieval organisation of Aylsham are important in understanding the sources that have been used.

The major manor of Aylsham was termed Aylsham Lancaster from about 1371, because it was part of the possessions of the Duchy of Lancaster, and Aylsham became the principal town of the Duchy in Norfolk. This was the largest of the Aylsham manors, and probably represents the bulk of the early pre-conquest unit or 'estate' that may have existed in late Saxon times. The northern part of the parish of Aylsham, in the main north of the Bure, formed a second manor that belonged, about 1200, to the Abbey of Bury St Edmunds, and was presumably granted to Bury by the King out of his great manor. Some parts of this manor did reach across the river. After the Dissolution of the Monasteries in 1538 the Bury Manor was bought by Edward Wood, Mayor of Norwich in 1548, and the manor became known as that of Aylsham Wood. Finally, the vicarage of Aylsham also had a small manor attached to it, and its holdings were scattered through the town. The surviving records of the three manors of Aylsham Lancaster, Aylsham Wood and Aylsham Vicarage have all had to be consulted, as properties held of all the manors lay in Millgate, though the bulk of them were in the manor of Lancaster. The mill seems to have been within the main manor. Domesday (1086) refers to two mills, but the site of the second mill is not known with certainty.

Three other major sources have been used in reconstructing something of the more recent history of Millgate. The first was a large collection of deeds relating to those Millgate properties which had been collected by Mr Tom Bishop. These have been a major quarry for this study. They are referred to throughout as the 'Bishop Bundles' and their contents are listed at the end of this work.

Secondly, the census returns for 1821 and 1841–81 have all been examined for Millgate, and provide a detailed inventory of all the people living in the street at the census day in each documented year. The census returns do not, however, tell us about those who left Millgate in the nineteenth century. We do not know, for example, if many families migrated to find work in the industrial towns of Midland and Northern England, or emigrated to Australia or the New World.

In addition, wills of the more prosperous members of the community up to 1857 have also been a valuable source, and help to throw light upon the details of at least some families. Sadly, inventories of household goods are of little help after about 1750.

One or two collections of family papers relate at least in part, to Millgate. Those of the Clover family have proved particularly interesting in revealing the business and family affairs of Joseph Clover, the portrait painter.

The records of Aylsham parish church are also of great value, but they have to be combed through in order to find items of particular relevance. Much has had to be discarded, interesting though it may be in other contexts.

Finally, there is the Aylsham town archive, housed in the Town Hall, which has a great deal of important material that has been accessible to the members of the group.

Numbers 3 and 5, Millgate

2

Millgate: the scene today

Millgate, from the site of the old gasworks down to the river crossing, is a typical ancient way. It was the way to the mill as well as a way leading out of the town to manorial fields, villages beyond, and eventually the coast. As an ancient way it winds slightly, dropping gently downhill, and has many buildings standing on the edge of the roadway. There are no pavements, and the various frontages are staggered, often according to their age. The whole effect is of unplanned pleasantness and informality.

This effect has much to do with the use of local building materials. Clay for bricks and tiles was available locally. Other roofing materials were thatch of heather which grew – and still grows – on the open commons hereabouts, and reeds and sedge from the river marshes and the broads. Some of the older houses are timber-framed from local trees. Flint pebbles, brought from the beaches on the coast, were used in a very decorative way in the houses of the early nineteenth century when transport became easier. The use of pebbles of a regular size gives an unexpectedly pleasing effect, contrasting with the quoins of white-painted brick which make up the outline of the building. Numbers 3, 5, 7 and 9 are splendid examples of this style, with their sash windows set in a regular pattern, gable and chimney stacks and neat tiled roofs.

Numbers 3 and 5 are a pair, and sport an interesting centre panel based on a curving swastika design in flint. These early nineteenth century properties stand well back from the road with good front gardens, which enables one to get the full benefit of their trimness. Other properties using the same style and materials are Number 20 (on the east side) which uses small flint pebbles, and the row of cottages built by Mash and dated 'W.E.M. 1845'. These are three cottages with irregularly spaced windows, those on the ground floor having unusual cambered heads. They have small front gardens, but very long gardens run back to the rear. It is good to see that the old type of red telephone kiosk has been retained alongside them.

In between these pebble-fronted dwellings there are colour washed taller buildings which show signs of many alterations, but have value as a group. Below Number 20 is another recently altered property that was formerly the last shop in Millgate. A row of buildings stretching back from here may have included some with light industrial uses.

Opposite these properties, at the top end of Millgate, is the island formed by New Road (an old part of Town Lane) and Bure Way (formerly Commercial Road, formerly Workhouse Lane). This contains a jumble of brick built properties, with Sycamore House, with its date stone of 1815, looking firmly down the hill. New Road has some smallish houses, including Garner's Cottages dated 1869. There is also a solid Victorian Chapel built by the Methodists (Wesleyan Reform) which has passed through several denominations; having now outlived its original purpose, the chapel has been converted into a private house. Just below this is a flint-faced property which shows the scars of having been a butcher's shop. At the back of these premises was the site of the earliest workhouse in Aylsham.

Passing down this part of the street, the next prominent building is on the east side, and is the Stonemason's Arms, which was converted into a private house in 2001. Its stone quoins, string course and slate roof and regular frontage indicate a Victorian style for this solid-looking hostelry. Below the Stonemason's Arms there is more Victorian building: a pair with the datestone 'Victoria Place 1851' with dormer windows, alongside some smaller properties of uncertain age.

Mill Row is a dead end leading to the water mill on the River Bure and to the Belt Farm. At one time several small cottages lined the beginning of the south side. Now there are gaps, and the ancient timber structures can be seen clinging to adjoining walls. There has also been some recent larger domestic building which leads to a contrast of old world charm and modern neatness. There is also infilling in the large garden of the Mill House. Nearer the Mill there is a long group of houses which form a pleasant secluded group in the presence of the bulk of the Mill itself, with the Mill House as the centrepiece with its solid brick indented quoins, probably dating from the eighteenth century. Although some of the other buildings show such alterations as filled-in archways and over-large windows, the general effect is bearable within the group.

The Mill itself is an imposing building straddling the River Bure. When it stopped working, in 1967, it had two interior wheels which are still in place, along with some of the milling machinery. The façade facing the mill pond formed by the river dates from the late eighteenth century, and is the latest of the many mills that have stood on this site since before 1086, the time of the Domesday Book. With its three storeys, with about ten windows on each floor and white painted projecting locum (for hoisting sacks) and white doors, it reflects well in the still water in front of it, whereas on the lower side, the water dashes out into the pool where the wherries used to load and unload straight from the mill itself. Now the twentieth century has caught up with this fine building, as the rear portion has been neatly converted into holiday flats, whilst the main building used to house a very large cinema organ which has subsequently been removed. The relationship between the River Bure, the Mill and the navigation is complex, and can best be explained by a diagram-cum-map.

Returning to Millgate itself, there are interesting buildings on the west side, just above the entrance to Mill Row. Numbers 15 and 17 form an L-shaped block, with Number 15 gable end on the road, and showing a fine set of a dozen windows or so, and an off-centre door with a neat canopy. There are also the remains of a moulded brick string course. Number 17 faces on to the road, and has an upper storey of roughly knapped flint, a simple door case, and a rough, squat stone cross on the north gable end.

The long building running back from the road is the Maltings, dated by a stone in the high gable end 'Robert Parmeter 1771'. Here grain, mainly barley, was steeped, allowed to sprout, then roasted to produce malt for brewing. The building has recently been converted into dwellings. Note the original upstanding ridge tiles provided for ventilation. The other similar block standing back and parallel to the road is modern, though built of re-used bricks and tiles. Opposite on the east side is Bure House. This imposing residence has a dated brick in its south wall incised with 'TR 1768'. It is of three storeys with large sashed windows and a central doorway with a pedimented door case with Tuscan pilasters. There is a brick string course and fine eaves decoration. The rear of the building has a surprising number of blank window openings, and a long orchard-like garden running back towards the mill with a good coped brick boundary wall that forms the north side of Mill Row. Bure House also has a curious two-and-a-half-storey lean-to wing butting on to the road. From here down to the bridge over the river, the road used to be lined with small cottages crowding along the roadside, as can be seen in old postcards from early in the last century, but only two or three small buildings now remain. On the west side, before the bridge, stands Bridge House, formerly the Anchor Inn. This is a large building of considerable character with many interesting details which include a fine door case and fanlight, good sashed windows, and three large dormer windows in a pantile roof. The north end, overlooking the river, is a large shaped gable in the Flemish style, built to impress when approached from the north.

Why the river crossing is situated here is not obvious, but here stood the *'great brygge over the Kings river at Aylesham . . . which brigge is a common passage for horse and carte both to the market at Aylsham and to the coaste for the countrie'* (PRO: Aug. Off. Misc. Books vol. 500, no. 196, quoted by Sapwell, *History of Aylsham*). This wooden structure was the responsibility of the parish. In 1547 church plate was disposed of, partly to cover repairs to the bridge, and also to avoid the parish losing the value of the plate. In 1759 the great bridge was replaced by the present brick structure, which bears the date and the name of the builder, W. Berry. This simple single arch has withstood several severe floods. The next, equally narrow, brick bridge was built in 1821, and is over the feeder to the Navigation, which also acts as a relief channel to the Mill.

Beyond this feeder channel stand Numbers 1 and 2 Mash's Row of 1848, facing the road, with red brick dressings containing a pebble flint frontage, and said to have been built as yet another inn. Numbers 3–8 follow on round the corner at right angles. Here Millgate merges into Drabblegate. The layout of the roads has changed several times since the arrival of the Navigation in 1779, the railway in 1880 and finally the by-pass in 1980. Dunkirk, and what was the lane leading to Tuttington, are now lined by modern mills and silos, industrial buildings, and estates sufficiently separated from the older charms and informality of Millgate itself to cause no clash between the old and the new.

3

An introduction to the people of Millgate

The people who appear in the next three chapters lived at a time when farming, and the trades and services associated with it, were relatively profitable. Yeomen farmers and grocers, millers and millwrights, a barber surgeon and a tanner were all able to afford copyhold land in Millgate, over and above what they had elsewhere. The eighteenth century saw many improvements in agriculture, and the outbreak of war with France in 1793 ushered in a period of even greater prosperity for farming. Although there was widespread rural unrest after 1815, prosperity returned in the 1830s, and continued until the 1870s. It is against this background that our families should be seen.

Each represents distinctive elements in the economic and social make-up of Millgate. Many who lived in Aylsham in the eighteenth century bought copyhold land in Millgate; James Curties is an example. He belonged to a well-established family of grocers who had been in that business for nearly a century. After his death in 1801, much of his land passed, indirectly, to John Fielde, a millwright, who accumulated a sizeable estate in Millgate by 1837. Another millwright, Thomas Harvey, also had land, and through his wife Ann was connected with the foundation of the first Baptist church in Aylsham.

Millgate attracted not only the inhabitants of Aylsham, but also people from neighbouring villages. John Power had been a farmer in Alby before he became a barber surgeon in the town, and John Wickes, father of William Wickes who bought the Belt estate in Millgate, was a tanner from Blickling. John Fielde the millwright came from Saxthorpe. The Mill itself was naturally the commercial hub of the area. After the opening to navigation of the River Bure between Coltishall and Aylsham in 1779, and the development of staithes, warehouses and boatyards, new opportunities for profit and employment presented themselves. Thomas Spurrell, miller and maltster, farmed land. The Parmeters who succeeded him did so too, but were also merchants and took an active part in the public life of Aylsham. William Mash continued the family tradition of farming, but combined it with being landlord of the Anchor Inn, and pursuing the building trade. Three generations of the Wright family were boatbuilders or watermen.

Whilst farming and milling remained lucrative occupations during the period, the story of these families shows a diversity of employment in the prosperous district of Millgate. This diversity is reflected in the types of houses which appeared in the area, ranging from the large homes of the prosperous traders and landowners to the humbler cottages of the people they employed.

Over the period we are exploring, many hundreds of people lived or worked or owned property in Millgate. Of the majority of these people we know nothing. In some instances we may know their names, but in most cases we do not even know that. These are the people that Ketton-Cremer describes so vividly in the introduction to one of his books:

> *As for the mass of the population, the workers in the fields, the wrights and smiths in the villages, the weavers and dyers and fullers in the towns . . . they have left little memorial of their lives and their toil. 'They took their wages and are dead'; and seldom, outside the pages of parish registers and parish accounts, can even their names be recovered.* (Ketton-Cremer, *Norfolk in the Civil War*, p. 30)

Without knowing their names, we can still know something of what they did and how they lived, their occupations and their recreations.

In Chapters 5 and 6 we will look at the Aylsham mills and some of the millers and millwrights who have been associated with the buildings.

In Chapter 7 we can obtain a picture of some of the unknown people of Millgate from the directories and census returns. Chapter 8 will allow us to look in greater detail at some of the people who were more fully recorded; those people, who for one reason or another, left some mark of their passing. These are the people who, being recorded in legal documents as owners of properties, partners in sales, inheritors of land, or simply through their profession, left a record that brings their lives up to the surface from out of the mass of the unknown.

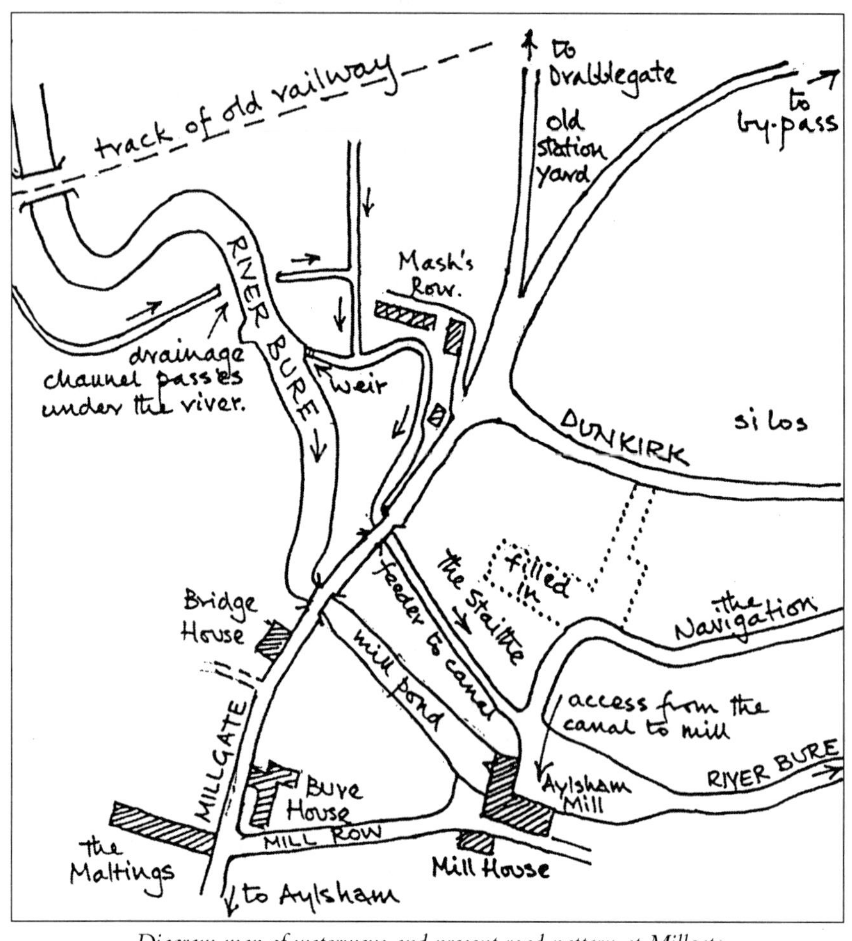

Diagram map of waterways and present road pattern at Millgate

4

The Navigation and the Staithe

The idea of making use of the River Bure (or the North River, as it was sometimes called) goes back a long way in the history of Aylsham. Sapwell, in his history of the town, quotes from the churchwardens' accounts of 1708–10 the expenditure of the considerable sum of £13 9*s* 4*d* for 'viewing and measuring the river to make it navigable'. The river is tidal up to Coltishall, and the Romans exported large quantities of pottery from Brampton, by water, down to the coast.

It would seem that the idea of speculating in making the river navigable drew several of the local landed gentry together to obtain an Act of Parliament for the construction of five locks and the digging of new channels to cut off sharp bends. The Act was obtained in August 1773 at a cost of £304 3*s* 2*d*. The Commissioners sworn in included the names of Walpole, Buckingham, Thos. Durrant, A. Marsham, Thos. Robins, Jno. Smith, J. Gay, James Curties and a Mr. Pepper (a miller at Buxton). They expected the cost of construction to be about £6,000, and an engineer by the name of H. A. Biodermann produced an excellent plan of the scheme, dated 1772, and took over the laying out of the 'land to be staked out'. Samuel Robinson, a contractor, undertook to do most of the work for £4,200, but failed to turn up to direct the work, and Biodermann was appointed to take charge.

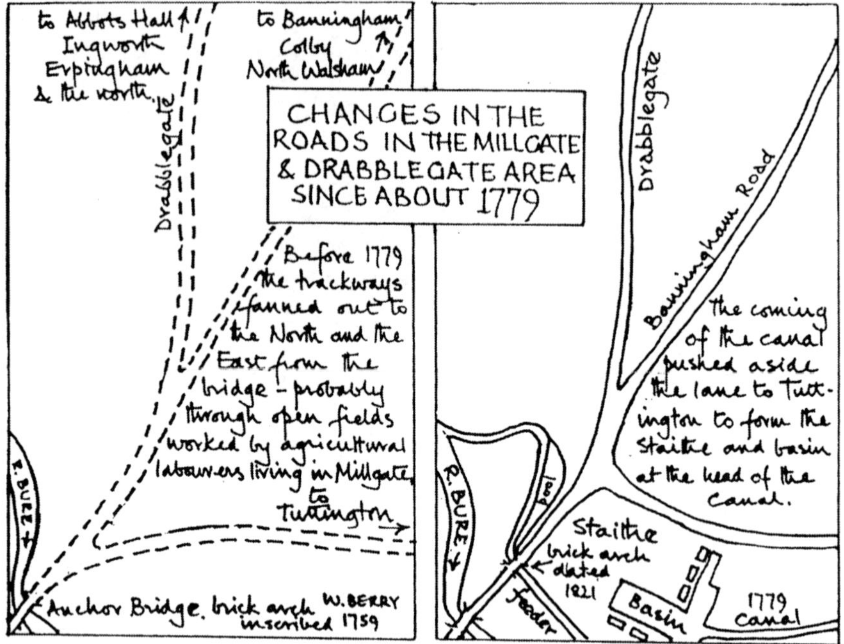

The early accounts are very detailed, and payments show that the money was running out as the considerable alterations to the course of the river at Burgh were undertaken by local builders and gangs of workmen paid by Biodermann. It would seem that this was as big an engineering undertaking as this part of rural Norfolk had ever seen.

The Commissioners met alternately at the Black Boys in Aylsham market place and the Dog Inn, which stood at the top of the Norwich Road, and dealt as best they could with the need for more and more money. In 1778, a new contractor was found to finish the constructional work. John Smith signed the agreement with a flourish on the map of the canal alongside many of the signatures of the Commissioners. However, by August of 1779 John Smith had decamped, leaving the work unfinished, and advertisements placed by the Commissioners in newspapers in London and York failed to locate him.

The Navigation was completed to the Staithe at Aylsham in late 1779, and brought prosperity to Millgate and Aylsham. At a time of bad local roads, the ability to transport heavy loads quickly and cheaply was a great asset. Wherries had traded on the Broads, where every village had a par-

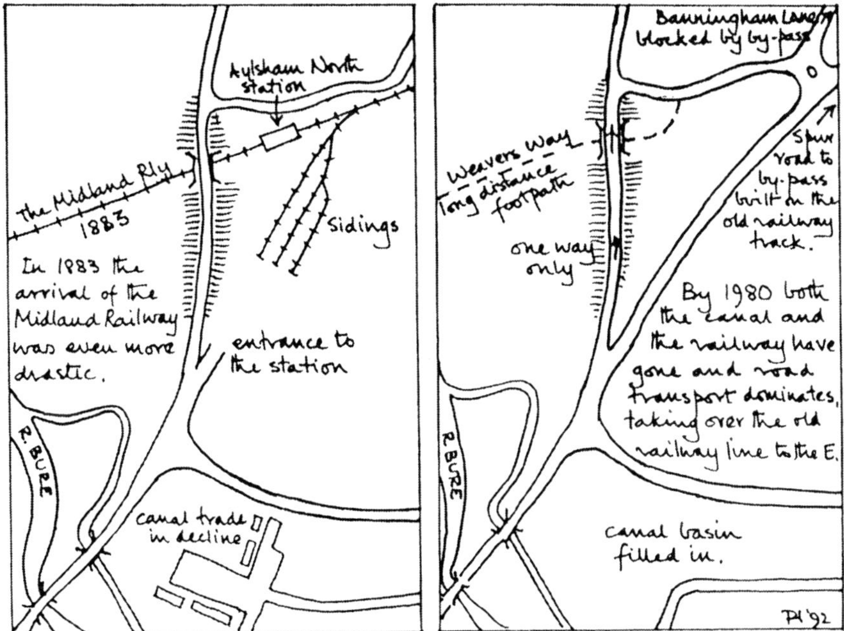

ish staithe. Loads could be taken down to Yarmouth, and transhipped for the coastal trade. The Navigation connected Aylsham to the Broads, and was designed to be used by the wherries under sail. The wherries were of 16 tons burden and drew 3½ feet (a metre or so) of water. There was no tow path, and locks were broader than on other waterways. Until recently, there were some who could remember seeing the great sails gliding quietly through the countryside.

Aylsham Staithe became a busy place, and expanded greatly from Biodermann's original oval 'Key' (as marked on his map) which was built on land owned by Edmund Jewell. Extra basins were added and warehouses built. As well as the transport of goods in and out, there was the repair and building of wherries. Those who worked at the Staithe lived in Millgate, and families of wherrymen resided there over many generations. There was also work to be done on the maintenance of the canal, which tended to silt up. Constant 'didling' (dredging) and weed cutting had to be done, and bridges and locks suffered from damage.

The goods transported varied greatly – some now seem strange and unknown – and from the toll books the following have been noted:

Barley	Coals	Fish salt	Flour	Pollard	Wool
Maize	Seed	Beans	Gravel	Manure	Malt
Osiers	Hay	Wheat	Cinders	Deal timber	
Scales (Meal?)		Cake	Marl	Billet*	

(*small twigs and bark for curing fish)

Passengers were taken down to Yarmouth and back. It must have been a pleasant way to travel compared with the jolting journey by road. The Navigation never made great profits for its promoters, probably because the initial expenditure had been so high. Tolls taken between 1780 to 1790 were, for example:

£	£	£
1780 – 177	1784 – 222	1788 – 265
1781 – 275	1785 – 169	1789 – 208
1782 – 316	1786 – 278	1790 – 215
1783 – 278	1787 – 259	

Under the original Act of Parliament manure and marl were not charged tolls, but the wherrymen had to be watched: on 3rd April 1780 one Jarvis was fined £5 for giving a false account of his lading. Many of the cargoes were connected with milling and with local crops. Although the owners of the five mills along the river (Horstead, Buxton, Oxnead, Burgh and Aylsham) all objected originally to the making of the Navigation, on the whole they eventually benefited, using their own wherries to transport goods to and from their mills. There were disputes about the use of water for turning their mill wheels, and the use of water to fill the various locks, which were nearly all at mill sites. Marker stones were set in the river bank to determine the water levels.

However, the Navigation did benefit the area through which it ran, transporting materials for agriculture – manure, lime, marl – as well as for local industries. Frederick Starling, a basket maker, remembered in 1860 agents from the great Yorkshire wood firms going round the neighbouring estates to buy up very large oak trees for shipbuilding. Gangs of Yorkshire working men lodged with cottage people in Millgate whilst they cut up the timber and loaded it on to wherries to be taken down to Yarmouth for shipment to the north of England.

At the beginning of the nineteenth century, wherrymen were paid by the voyage. The headman or captain got 35 shillings for a round trip from Aylsham to Yarmouth and back (40 miles). He had to find a capable hand to work under him. The voyage took, on average, a week, with fair winds (which came free!), but three return voyages might be made in a fortnight. At that time, an average of three wherries left Aylsham every week, but by that time the canal trade had been hit by the railways which had arrived in the 1880s. The goods yard of the Midland Railway was within a stone's throw of the canal staithe – probably put there on purpose. By 1904, the annual tolls had declined from £404 in 1893 to £278, and the canal owners were trying hard to reduce their costs whilst maintaining a useable waterway.

The end came in 1912, when an immense flood swept down the Bure valley, washing away weirs and locks, altering the channel of the river, and destroying and damaging the bridges. The Commissioners had no money to reinstate the Navigation, and had no response to their appeals for help to various government bodies. The Great War hindered any recovery, and the disposal of the remains lingered on until 1928 when the County Council finally, and reluctantly, agreed to the transfer of the little remaining property into its care. Nowadays, the locks have been adapted to control the flow of the water down the river; much of the Staithe at Aylsham has been filled in, though some old buildings remain standing, and the River Bure still flows placidly on, perhaps pondering on man's attempt to make use of its clear waters.

Aylsham water mill from Mill Lane

5

Aylsham water mill and some of its millers

It seems certain that a water mill has been in existence for many centuries near the spot where Millgate crosses the river Bure; possibly since Saxon times. There are two mills recorded in Domesday, the other probably being the mill at Bolwick. About 1190, the Millgate mill was granted to the Abbot of St Edmundsbury as part of Sexton's Manor, but by 1370 it had reverted to the Crown, and was let to a series of tenants. Its history remains fairly obscure until the seventeenth century, when the mill featured in a series of lawsuits, and through the records of these disputes the names of some of the owners or tenants emerge. In 1648 the mill was let to Captain Doughty for £60 per annum. A Tithe Court held at the Black Boys on 13th June 1682 'elicited some evidence as to the rights of the Vicar to tithes from the mill'. It also throws up some names – Richard Bloome, miller, stated that he had known the mills for over 50 years, and had heard that John Neave had farmed them at a rent of £100 a year, and that Mark Throry farmed them at £70 or £80. All the defendants in the suit had been successive occupiers of the mills, and whilst they had been there '*the mills were well wrought, and did grind great quantities of corn and grain*' (will of Thomas Spurrell, quoted by Jane Nolan in Aylsham Local History Society *Journal and Newsletter* 3 (1991), p. 55).

For those few years the occupiers of the mills had been:

William Purdy	1670–71
William Throry	for about a year
Bartholomew Wilkes	1675–78
Robert Sexton	until 1680
Miles Baispoole	in 1683 gave Robert Doughty £3,750 for the mill and its lands.

This Robert Doughty was the son of an earlier Robert Doughty who had held the mill for 20 years before settling it on his son in 1673 on his marriage. William Smyth was a tenant from 1696 to 1699, and in his time the mills were ruinous and required an outlay of £100 to make them tenantable.

Thomas Spurrell

Our knowledge of individual millers in the eighteenth century starts with Thomas Spurrell, who is described in documents as a miller in Aylsham as early as 1743. He had considerable properties in and around the town, and is buried in the central aisle of the nave in St Michael's church. Thomas Spurrell seems to have had no family apart from a brother, who was a baker in Norwich, and a number of nephews and nieces. In his will of 1771 he expressed the wish that 'all those my water mills, called Aylsham mills and their appurtenances' and all his other properties (not itemised) should be sold, and the proceeds and his personal effects shared amongst these relatives and his housekeeper, Mary Hammond. She and Thomas Harvey, a millwright, of Aylsham and Joseph Ames, miller at Hellesdon, were his executors. His final wish was:

> *On the day of my burial, the bells may ring in the manner as they did for the burial of Mr Edmund Jewell recently, and that the Aylsham ringers ring the Bumbled peal.*

According to the *Shorter Oxford English Dictionary*, this does not mean a muffled peal, as one might expect, but a booming note – 'a loud, deep resonant sound'.

The Parmeter family

The death of Thomas Spurrell coincided with the coming of the Canal Age and a new era for Millgate. The Aylsham Navigation Act was passed in 1773. Some of the key figures now emerging on the Millgate scene are those of Robert Parmeter and his children and grandchildren. Exactly when the Parmeter family came to own the Aylsham mill is not clear, but by 1763 Robert was paying the Poor Rate for Aylsham mill. When Thomas Spurrell died in 1771, Robert Parmeter bought some of his copyhold properties, including what was later to become the Anchor Inn, and he may well also have acquired the mill at this time.

In 1771, Robert Parmeter built the maltings, and around this time he also invested money, reported to be £200, in the Navigation 'advanced on the credit of the tolls'. From this time onwards the Parmeters steadily acquired property, mostly in and around the Millgate area but also in

The Maltings

Three generations of Parmeter millers

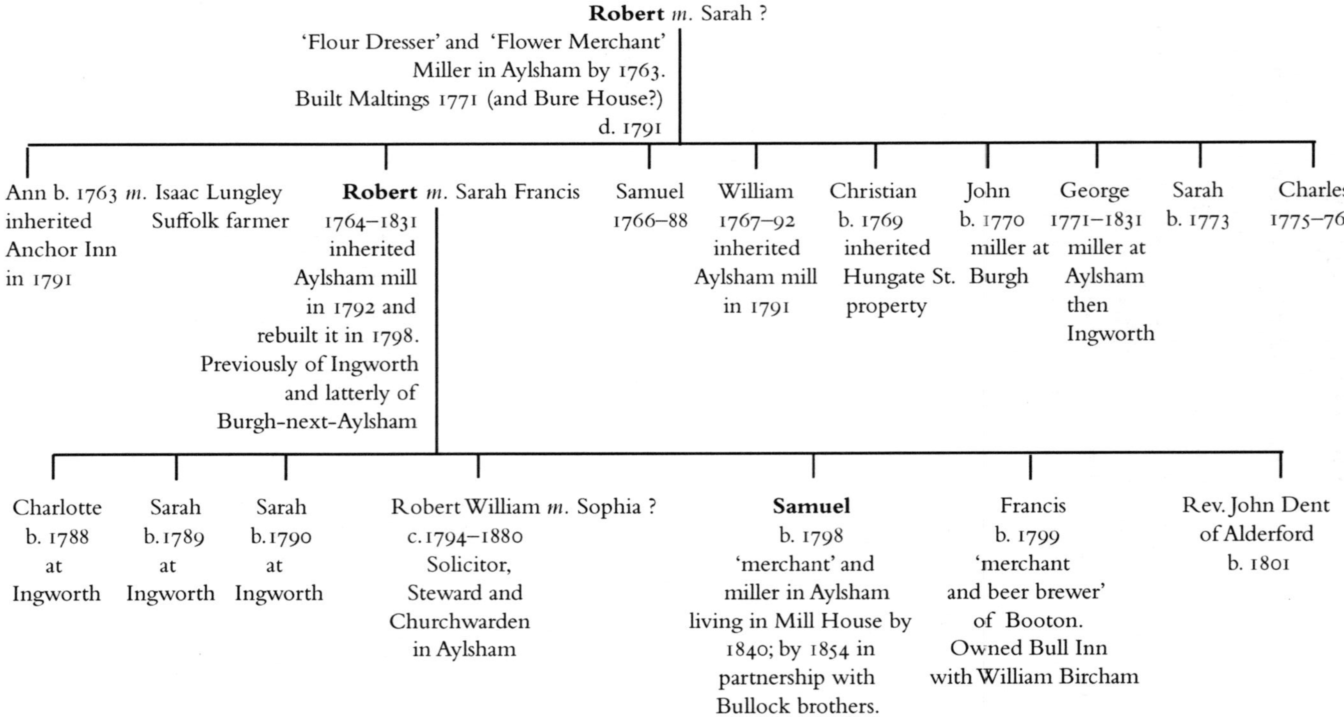

Hungate Street and elsewhere in Aylsham. There are regular entries in the Manor Court Books of Aylsham Wood and Lancaster from this time until well into the nineteenth century, although these are not always readily identifiable.

Robert the Elder died in 1791 leaving his Hungate Street property to his unmarried daughter, Christian, and the Anchor Inn to his married daughter, Anne Lungley. The rest went to his second son, William, who sadly died two years later, of consumption, leaving his recent inheritance to his brother, Robert. Robert was the miller at Ingworth, and it seems that he took over the Aylsham mill, but may have continued to live at Ingworth for some time, as his older children were baptised in Ingworth church. His brothers, George and John, became millers in Ingworth and Burgh respectively. William's will shows the extent of the property he inherited from his father:

> *I give and devise all that my messuage and dwellinghouse wherein I now dwell, together with the malthouses, granaries, houses outhouses, yards, gardens, orchards, lands and grounds . . . being in Millgate Street in Aylsham . . . to Robert Parmeter, my brother. Also, subject as afore-said, I give all that my estate and interest and terms of years yet to come and unexpired, of and in, all that staithe, yard, grounds and bank with the warehouses, houses and buildings erected in part of the same situate, standing, lying and being next Aylsham Navigation, and also all those my subscriptions or shares of £220 lent and advanced on the credit of the tolls of the said Navigation, by the said Robert Parmeter, my father, deceased, and all interest to my brother, Robert.*

Robert's inheritance was made conditional on his allowing their mother, Sarah, to continue to live in their house '*in whatever rooms she chooses*'. He also left £100 to each of his brothers and sisters.

Robert the Younger seems to have been able, shrewd and energetic. He was described by Arthur Young, on his travels, as 'a good farmer, and a very intelligible man'. He acquired further property near Aylsham river in 1795, and a year later, the extensive Millhouse properties on Mill Row, which Thomas Harvey, the millwright and executor of Thomas Spurrell's will, had taken up in 1771. This was in the form of three adjoining messuages or dwelling houses, at one time the home of Thomas Spurrell and his housekeeper, Mary Hammond, then of Thomas Harvey, and now the home of Sarah Parmeter, with barns, stables, carthouses and other buildings, yards and gardens, containing, in all, two acres. Later, these are described as the Millhouse, with a cottage on the west and a counting house on the east. There were also more distant portions of meadow land, near the Aylsham to Tuttington Road.

In 1798, the mill was rebuilt in its present form. In 1804, he bought a further two acres of land between the Navigation and the river, and two years later, land which seems to abut on to the present Bure House property – possibly the 'double cottages' of later documents.

He married Sarah Francis, a member of a well-known Aylsham family. They had four children: Robert William, Samuel, Francis and Rev. John Dent. Of these, it was Samuel who became the next generation miller. It is not known whether, as a family, Robert and Sarah lived in one of the family houses (Bure House and the Mill House) and, if so, for how long. At some stage they moved to Burgh-next-Aylsham, and he and Sarah are buried in Burgh church.

Samuel's older brother, Robert William, became a solicitor, and he and his wife, Sophia, seem to have contributed much to the life of the town and the church. They lived in the house now called Parmeters, in Cromer Road, and are remembered in the church by a plaque in the wall of the choir, and the gift of 'a warming apparatus' for use in inclement weather, given by their daughter, about 1880.

Although the Parmeter family held the mills for many years, from roughly 1771 to the middle of the nineteenth century, the mills were actually advertised for sale by auction in 1795. Ownership clearly never left the Parmeter family, but the auction notice in the *Norfolk Chronicle* for 26th September 1795 gives a useful picture of the extent of the property concerned:

> *To be sold by auction by Robert Ansell, at the Black Boys in Aylsham on Tuesday 6th October next at 3 o'clock in the afternoon* ... *the following estates in Lots.*
>
> **Lot 1.** *All those large and valuable water corn mills called Aylsham mills, with two water wheels, one with counter motion, the other Spurr; with four pair of French stones, four flour mills, two rolling screens together with all the going gears, irons, brasses and appurtenances belonging to the said mills, also three stables, granary, barn, wagon lodge and other convenient buildings near the mills, in very*

good repair; with gardens and pightle adjoining, containing about 2 acres.

A very good and convenient messuage, pleasantly situated near the mills, and fronting the river with gardens adjoining now in the use of Mrs Parmeter.

Also a new-built dwelling house adjoining the last, in the occupation of Mr William Cook.

And a very good cottage near the mills, very convenient for a servant of the miller to live in.

These mills are now in the occupation of Mr Parmeter, without lease; are well situate for trade, being at the head of the Navigation **. . .** *etc.*

Lot 2. *A Close of very good arable land, next the highway leading from Aylsham to North Walsham containing about 5 acres.*

Lot 3. *A Close of arable land containing about 2a. 2r. next the Kings Highway leading from Aylsham to Tuttington.*

Lot 4. *A Close of meadow or pasture, called the Furze meadow, next the said road leading to Tuttington, containing about 5a. 1r. 34p. more or less.*

Lot 5. *A Close of very good meadow land, called Bears meadow, containing about 4a. 2r. 16p. next the said road leading to Tuttington.*

Lot 6. *Another meadow adjoining the last, containing about 3a. 2r. 33p.*

All the above lands are lying in Aylsham aforesaid, at a short distance from the mills, and now in the use of the said Mr Parmeter without lease.

Lot 7. *A very good staithe, near the head of the Navigation, 75 ft. long with a large warehouse lately built upon it, brick and tiled with double floor, very convenient for a merchant.*

The Bullock brothers

Samuel Parmeter, in *White's Directory* of 1845, is described as corn miller and maltster, and proprietor of a wherry service to Yarmouth along with Messrs Copeman and Soame. He seems to have had no children, and went into partnership with John Thornton Bullock and his brother Stanley, finally selling out to them in 1856. They bought, and almost immediately mortgaged for £5,000 (with interest at 5% per annum), the freehold property of the water mills, mill dam and mill pool, dam meadow, the maltings and some other land, and the extensive copyhold properties including the Mill-house and cottages and counting house, Bure House and the double cottages to the north. Later on, they were allowed a further £2,000 mortgage on the properties.

By 1889 they were heavily in debt, apparently due to John Thornton Bullock's inefficiencies. William Forster, the Aylsham solicitor, became trustee of all the Bullock properties and responsible for paying off debts, while Stanley Bullock became manager of the business. An indenture of 1893 tells us that debts had been paid off, without sale or surrender of properties. These properties, both freehold and copyhold, were conveyed to Stanley Bullock.

Both brothers were dead by 1914, and a little later the mill was bought by Barclay, Pallett & Co.

Walter William Pallett

6

Barclay, Pallett and Press

Barclay, Pallett & Co., the new owners of the mill, already owned the Dunkirk Roller Mills which they had purchased in 1907. Walter William Pallett was born at Lodge Farm, Stevenage on 28th August 1855. He came to Norfolk when apprenticed to Press Brothers, Corn & Seed Merchants, of Spa Common, North Walsham. Eventually he became a partner, and the name of the firm was then changed to Press & Pallett, but on the death of Edward Press in 1906 Mr W. W. Pallett became the sole proprietor. He reorganised the firm and later the Barclay family entered the business and the name changed again to Pallett Barclay & Co. At this time the company had its head office at North Walsham with trading premises at North Walsham, Bacton Wood, Felmingham, Wayford Bridge, Cromer, Gunton and Cawston.

In 1907, when the Dunkirk Roller Mills came on to the market after Ben Cook had retired, it was purchased by the company who formed a second company called Barclay Pallett & Company Ltd. Mr Robert Leicester Rust, who had worked for Mr Pallett since 1900, was sent to Aylsham as the manager. After Walter William Pallett died in 1913 the two companies were merged. At the same time they purchased the Wroxham Mills and the whole company was then known as Barclay Pallett & Co. Ltd.

Dunkirk Roller Mill

The roller mill was situated between the Tuttington Road and the canal at

Aylsham and dates back to 1856 when Frederick Copeman was the owner. It was purchased by Benjamin Cook in 1878, who already owned mills at Itteringham and Blickling, which he had already improved. When Benjamin Cook purchased the mill it contained four pairs of millstones. In 1886, Cook installed a four sack/hour roller mill plant – the first in the district. Three years later, he built offices, seed granary and stabling beside the road, enclosing the yard. Alongside the canal and forming the fourth side of the yard was the building known as the Bone Mill and the area by the mill was still known by this name.

In 1878, a Mr Vince carried on trade in bone meal, meat meal and other associated products. Mr Cook acquired the land and buildings before building the new offices. In 1894 Cook added wheat washing and drying machinery, and carried out other changes. The first exhibition of roller milling machinery (as opposed to the long established millstone) took place in the Royal Agricultural Hall in London in 1879. It was then that English millers started to convert to the new system of milling; so Mr Cook was in the forefront of modern milling techniques. For nearly 30 years there was a good flour trade.

After Cook retired in 1907, Barclay Pallett purchased the mills at an auction held by Messrs Irelands in Norwich on Saturday 6th July 1907. Three lots were offered:

Lot 1. *The steam Roller flour mills, together with wheat cleaning plant, offices, granary and stabling.*

Lot 2. *Double dwelling House (opposite)*

Lot 3. *Double dwelling House (opposite)*

The company purchased Lot 1 and trading carried on without a break. Plans were made to improve the milling plant, but these were not carried out. An agreement was made with the Post Office to install a telephone at an annual rent of £7 10*s* 0*d* to cover 480 calls. In 1910, Henry Simon the milling engineers improved the flour milling plant. There is a group photograph of mill employees and engineers taken at this time.

The company owned and used a number of wherries and an agreement was made in 1909 with the Aylsham Canal Company to pay an annual fee of £50 in lieu of all tolls on the canal. In 1910, the 28th Annual Milling

Convention was held at Cromer; it was the only time this convention was ever held in Norfolk, so it was an important occasion. The souvenir issue of *Milling* magazine contained write-ups of many mills in East Anglia, including Aylsham.

In 1912, catastrophe overtook the canal, the river and the mill. On 27th August six inches of rain fell in 24 hours causing serious flooding of the Bure valley. R. L. Rust recalled that he went home at 6 o'clock in the evening, and was called back at 6.30 pm. The water level had risen two feet in a half-hour, due to the M. & G. N. railway embankment collapsing and allowing a surge of water to flow downstream. Locks and brick-arched bridges were swept away, and mills and houses flooded. No damage was caused to the machinery, but many sacks of grain and flour were damaged. Some wherries were trapped at Aylsham, and were taken down the canal and river when water levels were high enough. At Buxton, they were taken out of the river, and manhandled across the road to reach safe water below the mill. With the coming of the railways to Aylsham in the middle of the 1880s, use of the canal had declined. Damage caused by the flood was not repaired, and navigation ceased on the upper reaches of the river Bure above Horstead mill after August 1912.

In June 1914, Aylsham water mill came on the market, and Barclay Pallett & Co. purchased the mill at auction, so they now owned both Aylsham mills, using one for flour manufacture and the other for animal food manufacture. In August 1914, the Great War started, and the Ministry of Food took over responsibility of flour manufacture with the mill being run by the company for the Ministry.

At the end of the war, the control of the flour mill was handed back to the company, and suitable compensation was given. With this money, the company re-modelled the wheat cleaning and drying plant, and also updated some of the roller mill plant. The work was carried out by E. R. & F. Turner, milling engineers of Ipswich.

When remodelling the wheat-cleaning plant, the roof of the building was raised, the locum removed and the smaller of the two tall chimneys demolished. All this took place in 1920, and a photograph shows the mill as it was before these alterations took place.

Aylsham water mill

The water mill was purchased by the Parmeters, and rebuilt in its present form in 1798; later it belonged to the Bullock brothers and in 1914 came on to the market with land, houses and cottages in Millgate. A copy of the sale catalogue gives the date of sale as 16th June 1914. The mill was bought by Barclay Pallett, and the two mills were managed by Mr R. L. Rust for the next 50 years. From the plan of the lots for sale, it is interesting to note how well the purchase of this property complemented the Dunkirk roller mills. The Company bought everything except:

R. L. Rust

Lot 2 Millgate House
Lot 3 Bure House
Lot 4 Millgate Cottages
Lot 7 The Malthouse
Lot 8 Meadow
Lot 10 Shop, bakehouse, windmill and dwelling house.

Robert Leicester Rust subsequently purchased the Malthouse, for there was an agreement to let land adjacent to the Malthouse to the War Office for the purpose of erecting a bath-house for troops. The agreement was dated 19th May 1916, Mr Rust also purchased Millgate House a little later. In 1918 he moved there, following Colonel W. Purdy who moved to Woodgate House.

During the Great War, the two mills and Wroxham mills, together with other trading sites, were profitably managed by the company. These sites were:

Bacton Wood Mill and granary
North Walsham station granary
Cromer station granary
Felmingham mill
Wroxham staithe granary
Cawston coal yard
Wayford Bridge granary

During the war employees serving in the forces were paid a part of their previous wages but employees working at the mills were paid a bonus. By 1922 there was a general down-turn in the economy, and employees were asked to accept a reduction in wages. Flour milling at Wroxham ceased, and Aylsham took over flour production and supplied Wroxham customers. Animal food production and general trade continued to be profitable, and wherries continued to ply from Bacton Wood, Wroxham and Wayford Bridge.

The first steam lorry was purchased just prior to the Great War, and continued in use for many years; a second lorry was purchased after the war. Petrol-driven lorries began to replace the horse and wagon, but horse-drawn coal carts still continued to be used until the end of the Second World War. Some of the drivers were Walter Johnson, Jack Wright, Tom Wright, Fred Grix, Reggie Gladman, G. Suffling and G. Eastoe.

At that time the flour mill was powered by a large twin cylinder steam engine which was used to drive the whole plant through a system of line shafts and flat leather belts. This engine was a 75 h.p. twin cylinder Richard & Watts with a Galloway boiler and the engine minders were Jack Matthews and George Eastoe. A Mr Smith ruled the workforce of a dozen men but the office was worked by an elderly gentleman named White who lived in one of the mill houses across the road, and turned up early each morning wearing a cloth cap and slippers.

Before the Great War flour was packed in 20 stone [280 lb] sacks. These were delivered by horse and cart to local bakeries, and usually carried on a man's back up some outside steps to the bakery loft. R. L. Rust told the story that when legislation was introduced to limit the weight of flour in a bag to 10 stone, the carters were very angry because it meant climbing the bakery steps twice as many times! Flour milling was never very flourishing, but trade continued with local bakeries and grocers' shops throughout the area, and as far away as London. Flour to London went by rail, and then subsequently by lorry. In the early 1930s, a small self-raising flour plant was introduced, and flour was packed in branded 3½lb [¼ stone] bags, and sent out in packs of a dozen. In 1920, the wheat cleaning and drying plant was remodelled by E. R. & F. Turner Ltd. of Ipswich, who also re-modelled the flour-milling plant, and there is mention of the plant standing idle for six months when under Flour Milling Control, just after the Great War.

The introduction of motor transport came slowly during the 1920s. Up to the introduction of mechanical transport, all cereals came to the mill from the farm by horse and wagon and at harvest time there could be up to 30 wagons waiting to be unloaded. The corn was either threshed in the field at harvest time, or stacked and threshed from the stack at a later date. It was then put into corn sacks and manhandled. When the sacks arrived at the mill they were either unloaded and carried on a man's back, or wheeled on a sack trolley and then stacked. Corn sacks would be provided by the miller, each sack holding a volume of grain which had been weighed on the farm:

Wheat	1 sack = 1 coomb = 252 lb
Barley	1 sack = 1 coomb = 224 lb
Oats	1 sack = 1 coomb = 168 lb

(Coomb is a Norfolk/East Anglian word)

English wheat, providing it was dry enough, was stored in sacks until required, then mixed with Canadian or American wheats for making bread flour, or milled on its own for soft flour. In 1929, the steam engine was replaced by a Ruston Hornsby (of Lincoln) twin cylinder diesel engine of 120 h.p., with a rope drive, and a new engine house was built. The steam engine was sold, but the boiler remained until it was removed to make way for a night-watchman's room during the Second World War. The tall chimney was removed in 1937. The period between the wars was a difficult time, with little change, and the fortunes of the company fluctuated, but the company was always profitable.

There was no mains electricity in Aylsham until 1931, so both mills generated their own. At the flour mill there was no electricity until the engine started each morning, and until then candles were used. This was a dangerous practice in an old wooden building, and even more dangerous in a flour-mill. The water mill used a system of accumulators which were recharged each day by a dynamo driven from the water-wheel. In 1931, when mains electricity came to the town, power was then available to run electric motors. It was not long before a small electrically powered hammer mill was installed in the water mill. Ground cereals became available for the manufacture of balanced rations for livestock.

Throughout the 1930s, this trade steadily increased, and two vertical mixers were installed in the water mill. Mill stones driven by water power continued in use for grinding farmers' corn and some malting barley was stored in corn sacks on the granary floor. An average of five men were employed and one of these men, Mr Harper, was skilled in dressing mill-stones. A tap, tap all day meant he was using a millbill, and chipping grooves into the surface of the millstone. The backs of his hands were black, caused by small flecks of stone embedding themselves in the skin of his hands. Naturally, it was always necessary to wear goggles to protect his eyes.

The flour mill continued production for either eight or 12 hours each day, and occasionally for 18 hours, but the flour trade was never good. As the sale of balanced rations increased, the sale of slab-cake decreased and eventually ceased altogether. Slab-cake was the residue from the extraction under pressure of oil from cotton seed, palm seed and linseed. The residues became a thick slab of about 1½ inches, 3 ft 6 in long and 15 inches wide. These were manhandled, stacked in tiers and eventually fed to cattle, but any farmer who used this feed also needed a cake-breaker. Modern methods, including the use of a solvent for oil extraction, terminated the production of slab-cake.

A trade developed in seed corn, artificial fertiliser sales increased, and small seeds (clover and grass) sales continued. General business conditions were improving, as the fortunes of agriculture became more prosperous.

World War 2

The start of the 1939–45 war brought in rationing of feeding stuffs, a limited supply of fertiliser, and control of flour milling by the Ministry of Food. Many employees were retained in reserved occupations or were too old to be called up and women were employed in the office; some of the older employees also served in volunteer services such as the Observer Corps, the Fire Service, the Home Guard, the St John Ambulance and the Red Cross.

The army built strong-points at strategic places. A concrete bag pill-box was built against the north end of the water mill, adjacent to the sluice-gate, which commanded views of the road bridge and the shallow water at the bottom of the mill pool. At this time, there was a small, single-plank footbridge across the river at the bottom of the mill pool, where there was a hard gravel bottom, and the water was shallow. The army decided, in the interests of security, that the footbridge should be destroyed.

The County Council owned buildings adjacent to the staithe, which were hired by the company. At the start of the war, the County Council terminated the lease and converted the buildings to decontamination sheds for use in case of chemical warfare. At the flour mill, the old boiler house was converted to a night-watchman's room, and throughout the war a man was always on duty.

After the war

For the first two or three years after the war, little change took place. Then, with steadily increasing labour costs, changes were necessary. A second and larger grinder was installed in the water mill. Farm chemicals began to appear, and the sale of fertilisers increased rapidly. Transport requirements increased, new lorries replaced old ones and the horse and cart disappeared. Bulk handling of corn became essential to reduce labour requirements. Four 50-ton bins were installed at Aylsham flour mill, and a facility for tipping sacks from the lorry into a small intake conveyor. This necessitated filling in the cutting from the canal to inside the mill building – a facility which had not been used since 1912. A warehouse and boiler house were also demolished.

In 1953 a complete remodelling of the water mill took place. The installation of a pelletting press and meal plant involved bringing into use the disused bottom floor beneath the granary floor, known as the Wood Shed. A small boiler house was erected at the east end with a bulk molasses tank below floor level. New style paper bags were used, and a big advertising campaign steadily increased sales of feeding stuffs.

In 1959 a grain silo and dryer was built at Dunkirk on land adjacent to the flour mill. This necessitated demolishing a pair of cottages. A weighbridge was installed; the turnover to bulk-handling of grain was rapid, and the use of corn sacks speedily decreased. For the first few years, use of the dryer was heavy but with the introduction of the combine harvester it became more economic for the farmers to have their own drying facilities. After a few years, most grain was being dried on the farm.

In 1966, the company decided to build a new provender mill alongside the silo, on land which belonged to the company and had previously been used as allotments. The grain silo could therefore supply both the flour mill and the new provender mill with all their grain requirements in bulk. Building commenced early in 1966 and production commenced in 1967. Animal feed production ceased at the water mill, at Wroxham and North Walsham. In 1967 the company was sold to British Oil and Cake Mills, a subsidiary of Unilever, and the new owners enlarged the plant and added bulk handling facilities. Production of BOCM foods commenced in 1969.

Eventually the flour mill ceased production and closed, and for a long time it was used by the local Fire Service for training. In 1975 the building was demolished to make way for a new building; which was used for the manufacture of premixes. The water mill was sold in 1969 to Mr J. Crampton, who converted part of it into holiday flats, and the front section over the river housed a theatre organ, later removed. The water wheel and machinery had been renovated and were in working order. British Oil and Cake Mills and Silcock Feeds, both national manufacturers of animal feeds and subsidiaries of Unilever, were merged into one company known as BOCM Silcock. The new company had a policy of closing the very large port mills, and building smaller, computerised mills throughout the country. Strategically placed, the aim was to be within 60 miles of any farm and one of these new mills was built at Bury St Edmunds, and it was not long before the company realised that the Bury mill could also supply Aylsham's customers.

With the introduction of milk quotas, and the downturn in animal food requirements, the closure of Aylsham was inevitable. Redundancy notices were issued to all employees in October 1984 and production of animal feeds ceased on 1st January 1985, but then the notices of redundancy were withdrawn and the plant was converted to the manufacture of fish food. Thus started a programme of specialisation at Aylsham mill. Premix manufacture continued, and when fish food manufacture was transferred to a new mill in Scotland other specialised foods were introduced at Aylsham, which had become the special foods plant for BOCM Silcock. Much money has been spent on plant at Aylsham and its future seemed assured. However, that was not to be. Business finally ceased at the mill on 31st January 1994 and the property sold to a developer. The water mill was preserved and is currently being altered to provide residential accommodation.

7

People and trades

The Millgate community, essentially a part of Aylsham, was divided from the town by a large area of open ground below White Hart Street, and this dividing swathe of countryside was continued eastwards by the Belt estate. The links between Millgate and the rest of Aylsham were by two roads: Town Lane, a turning off White Hart Street, and Gay's Lane (later renamed as Gas House Hill), which is a continuation of White Hart Street.

In the nineteenth century, although Town Lane was a narrow street, it appears to have been the more important of these two roads. However, road widening in the twentieth century reversed their status, and today it is a narrow one-way lane. These two roads eventually meet at the start of Millgate, just below the site where the gas works was eventually established in 1850.

We can learn much about the people of Millgate and their everyday life from the directories and census returns of the period. In 1821, 370 people lived in Millgate. This was a fifth of the population of Aylsham. As Aylsham expanded, Millgate remained much the same size for lack of space, and it housed a smaller percentage of the town's population, as the following figures show:

Year	*Pop. of Aylsham*	*Pop. of Millgate*	*%*
1821	1,853	370	20%
1851	2,741	352	12%
1871	2,505	339	14%
1881	2,674	410	15%

By the mid-nineteenth century, Millgate had three public houses: the Anchor, near the bridge, the White Horse, halfway up the hill, and the Stonemason's Arms opposite. John Freeman, who kept the Stonemason's, was a stonemason and at one stage employed four men and two apprentices in his yard beside the pub.

The river and the Navigation created considerable employment. The water power was harnessed to drive the two wheels of the large mill, which in 1851 was providing employment for 19 men. The water mill and the Navigation are described separately in Chapters 4 and 5, but it is worth repeating here what major sources of employment they were to Millgate and its people. In 1830 Robert Parmeter operated a regular wherry service from Millgate to Yarmouth. In 1845 the weekly service was shared between Samuel Parmeter, Copeman & Soame, corn and coal merchants in Dunkirk, and Thomas Shreeve, Corn, Cake and General Merchant, from the staithe at Millgate. It had developed by 1850 into a daily service and continued as such until the end of the century when once again it reverted to a weekly service, probably because of the competition from the railways.

Secondary trades also were created. The river wherries were the principal means of transport between Aylsham and the coastal ports, and consequently much of this secondary work was directly associated with the river trade. An average of 15 men were employed on the waterfront, but carters, hauliers, a wheelwright, harnessmaker and blacksmith were all closely associated with the waterways. Work on the waterfront continued in importance even after the arrival of the railways in 1880. It was the great floods of 1912 which destroyed all this when wherries were no longer able to reach Aylsham. Boat building and a boat repair yard had been established on the east side of the canal. This business, which was run by different generations of the Wright family and employed several workers, was lost at the same time.

One of the largest employers in Millgate was Robert Bartram, described as a master builder and farmer. He was also a stone and marble mason who also dealt in Staffordshire tiles. His father, William, also a builder, had been a carpenter, timber merchant and coal dealer. At one time the firm employed 26 men, ten of whom lived in Millgate.

However, agriculture always remained the largest source of employment throughout this period. One can understand this; fields and meadows reached almost into Millgate, and census returns show how closely Millgate people were connected to the land:

Principal occupations of male workers in Millgate

Year	*Agricultural*	*Watermen*	*Building*	*Milling*
1821	39	–	–	–
1851	51	7	11	8
1861	41	15	8	7
1871	36	12	6	4
1881	40	17	16	5

A basket maker employed five men, and in 1851 had two apprentices. Women were employed as servants, dressmakers, straw bonnet makers, cooks, shop hands, a laundress, milkwomen and a schoolmistress.

This part of Aylsham also housed the Workhouse, which served the whole parish. This was built in 1776 on part of the land left by Thomas Cressy 'for the use of the poor people of . . . Aylsham'. This Thomas Cressy was, in fact, the uncle of the Thomas Cressy mentioned by Sapwell as churchwarden in 1638. The charity he founded still exists today and the details of it are set out in his will of 1613 written two years before his death:

> *I doe give and devise unto Simon Smith, Robert Doughtie and John Barker of Ailsham aforesaid evermore All those my houses and tenements situate and beinge in Ailsham aforesaid in a street called Millgate Domicilia Called or known by the name of or names of Smith and Grickes contayning twelve small dwellings . . . for the use of the poore people of the said town of Ailsham.*

The will goes on to ensure the financing of this project by arranging for the rents and profits of lands and grounds adjoining these properties for repair and maintenance 'of the said houses forever'. He further directs that the 'overplus of the profitts' of the said lands and grounds which remain shall yearly be distributed to the said poor of Aylsham at the discretion of the churchwardens. When one of the trustees dies, 'the other two surviving are to choose another inhabitant of the said town to join with them in his stead and soe to continue from age to age forever'. He reiterates that 'the said twelve severall dwellings shall be from time to time maintained forever without sufferinge anie of them to be lettdown or impayred'.

When the workhouse was built later, it was capable of housing 100 inmates, but it usually held only a third of that number. Two cottages remaining were let and the income used to support the workhouse. In 1836 the Aylsham Union was formed and in 1837 the Aylsham workhouse was abandoned. The new Union workhouse was built in Cawston Road in 1849 to serve all 46 villages in the Union. This building is now St Michael's Hospital. During the period between the closure of the parish workhouse and the opening of the Union workhouse, the Aylsham needy were housed at Cawston and Buxton.

The parish workhouse building was still standing after its abandonment long enough to be recorded in Wright's 1839 map [schedule no. 298], so that we do know its precise location. It was demolished in 1842, and the land sold in 1856. The income from the investment of the proceeds is still distributed today as part of the combined parish charities.

By studying the census returns we can discover how many of the inhabitants of Millgate were natives of the town. More women came from outside the area than did men. Perhaps the men looked for a wife in the neighbouring villages. The 1871 census, used as an example, reveals the following pattern:

Place of birth	*Male*	*Female*
Aylsham	118	88
Adjacent parishes	2	21
Other parts of Norfolk	27	51
Norwich	6	5
Other counties	13	8
TOTALS	166	173

The few shops in Millgate were mixed businesses. The baker sold groceries, the stonemason was also the landlord of the Stonemason's Arms. Fish was cured and sold by the landlord of the Anchor Inn, who probably kept his fish in the fishponds at the rear of the inn, and the landlord of the White Horse was also the butcher, a slaughterer and a farmer.

Today, all the shops have vanished. Some have become houses, but their conversions betray their previous use, and the shape of the shop windows can still be detected. The water mill no longer functions as a mill, the butcher's shop and the timber yard have vanished and the gas works have closed. The Millgate Nurseries which had been established in 1929 were replaced by houses and bungalows in Stuart Road. The Anchor Inn, the White Horse and the Stonemason's Arms are all now private houses.

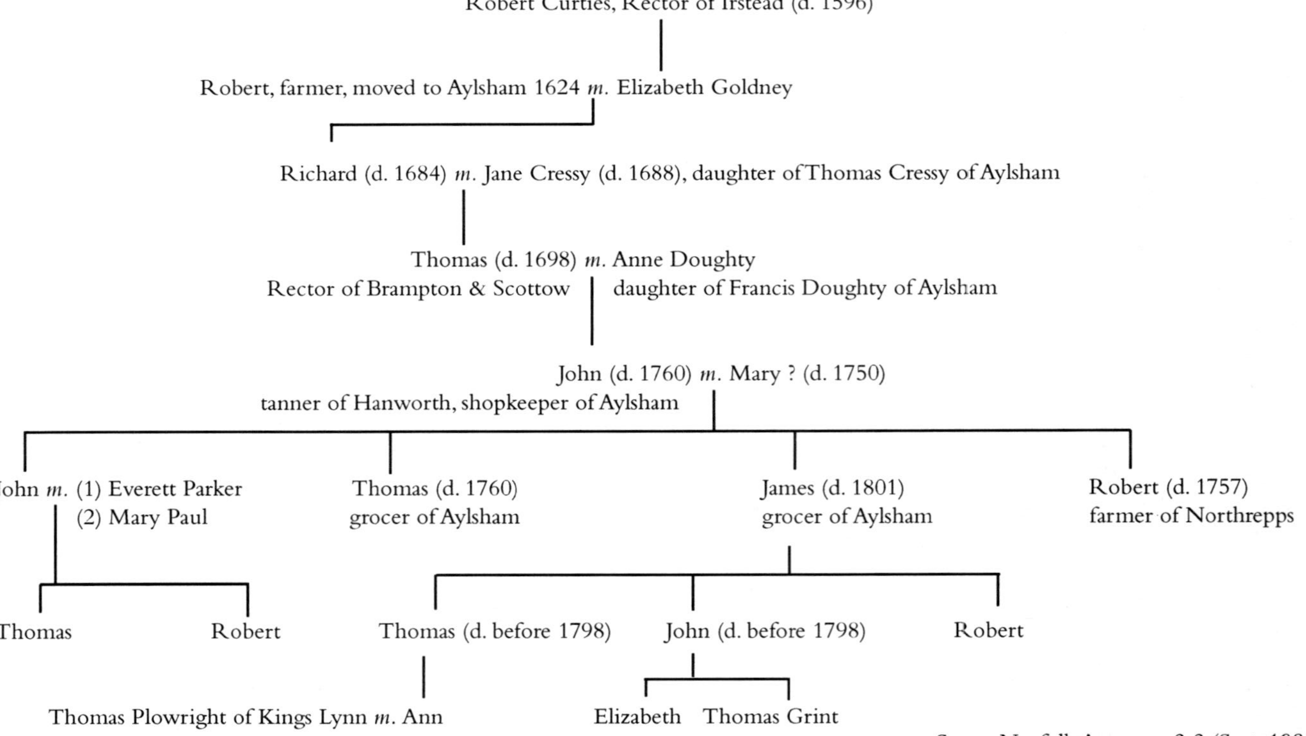
The Curties family
Robert Curties, Rector of Irstead (d. 1596)
Robert, farmer, moved to Aylsham 1624 m. Elizabeth Goldney
Richard (d. 1684) m. Jane Cressy (d. 1688), daughter of Thomas Cressy of Aylsham
Thomas (d. 1698) m. Anne Doughty
Rector of Brampton & Scottow
daughter of Francis Doughty of Aylsham
John (d. 1760) m. Mary ? (d. 1750)
tanner of Hanworth, shopkeeper of Aylsham
John m. (1) Everett Parker
(2) Mary Paul
Thomas (d. 1760)
grocer of Aylsham
James (d. 1801)
grocer of Aylsham
Robert (d. 1757)
farmer of Northrepps
Thomas
Robert
Thomas (d. before 1798)
John (d. before 1798)
Robert
Thomas Plowright of Kings Lynn m. Ann
Elizabeth
Thomas Grint
Source: Norfolk Ancestor 2:2 (Sept. 1980)

8

Some Millgate families

After looking at the people of Millgate in general, we can now turn to some specific personalities or families who were part of the Millgate scene.

James Curties

James Curties (1725–1801) was a member of a well-known Aylsham family. Robert, his great-great grandfather, had moved from Irstead to Aylsham in the early seventeenth century, and had bought lands from John Orwell, probably the man listed in the Rental as holding 'a mess. with its appurts ... built up in Myllgatestreete', one rood in area, in 1586. Robert himself appears in the Rental holding four acres of arable land in the East Field in the Millgate area in 1620. He is also the first Curties of many to be churchwardens of St. Michael's church, Aylsham.

The family continued to accumulate property in Aylsham in the next generation. Richard, Robert's second son, married Jane, daughter of Thomas Cressy. By the time he died in 1684, he owned the land called Orwells, property in Millgate, and 30 acres called Mucklins. (Munckeley in Eastonfield appears as a place-name in the rental.)

Richard's grandson, John Curties, whose memorial is on the floor of the nave in St Michael's church, was a weaver by trade. Later he became a grocer in Aylsham, and finally a tanner in Hanworth. He died in 1760, leaving a large family, including James, born in 1725, his third son.

While James's brothers became respectively a tanner (John junior), a grocer (Thomas), and a weaver (Robert), James, also described as a grocer, consolidated the family lands in Millgate. Among the Millgate documents there are papers relating to James's admission to two copyhold properties. The first, in 1766, is to ten acres, formerly owned by George Johnson, north of the River Bure and abutting upon the Aylsham to Tuttington Road, and the second, in 1773, is to three acres and one rood, formerly owned by Thomas Spurrell, miller. When Elizabeth Custans was in need of money in 1763, she mortgaged her estate to James Curties for £336, and in 1794, he was one of the Trustees of the Norwich to Cromer Turnpike Trust. He was clearly a man of substance.

James's will, drawn up in 1798, shows him taking great care in dividing his property among his nephews, great-nephews and nieces. He himself was a bachelor, and his brothers, John, Thomas and Robert, predeceased him. John's sons, Thomas and Robert, were given modest legacies. Robert's family had moved to Norwich and, on his death, moved again to Northrepps, where his widow remarried. It was the family of Thomas, James's second brother, who were the chief beneficiaries of his will, perhaps because James and Thomas were both grocers, and both, as far as we know, lived the whole of their lives in Aylsham. Thomas junior, the eldest son, was left £200, but died before his uncle, so his legacy went to his daughter, Ann, who had in addition £300 of her own. She married Thomas Plowright of King's Lynn, a member of the firm of ironmongers Plowright & Pratt. John, the second son, was also left £200, and also predeceased his uncle, so the sum was shared between his daughter Elizabeth and his son Thomas Grint Curties. Thomas senior's third son, Robert, had £150. The land which James had bought in 1766 and 1773 went to Stephen Ashley, a wine merchant of Aylsham, who had married one of James's nieces.

By the times James died in 1801, many of the younger generation had themselves died, or moved away from the town. The seventeenth and eighteenth centuries seem to have been the heyday of the Curties family in Aylsham and there were no Curties in Aylsham in the 1821 census.

The Harvey and Bane families

On the floor of the nave in St Michael's church there is a tablet recording the death on 9th June 1770 of Thomas Spurrell, miller. Part of his estate was sold in 1771 to Thomas Harvey, millwright. It was copyhold land held from the Lord of the manor of Aylsham Wood, and is described as

> *all that messuage situate in Millgate Street in Aylesham . . . next the King's Highway leading to the bridge on the part of the west, and the street or way leading to the water mills on the north part . . . with the yard pump and garden to the same belonging. And also the barn and stable adjoining the said messuage . . . containing by estimation, 1 rood more or less, and also, all that close of arable land called or known by the name of Maiden's Bower, lying and being in Aylesham, aforesaid, next a horseway, leading to a meadow of the said Manor, on the part of the east; and a meadow called Pope's meadow, on the part of the west, and abutting upon the King's Highway leading from Aylesham aforesaid to Tuttington towards the North, and upon lands of the Lord of the said Manor towards the south, containing by estimation 1 acre and 1 rood more or less.*

Thomas Harvey left these properties, and others which he had in Cromer, to his wife, Ann, for her lifetime. They were then to be sold by his executors, Thomas Drake of Aylsham, Gent. and John Pedder of Hevingham, farmer. From a memorial tablet in the Baptist chapel in Aylsham, we discover the relationship between Ann Harvey and John Pedder:

In a vault beneath this tablet are deposited the remains
of John Pedder, Gent. late of this parish
who died the 7th of January 1827 aged 78 years.
Also of Frances, his wife, who died
the 5th March 1831, aged 84 years.
And also of Ann Harvey, her sister, who died
the 16th August 1822, aged 83 years.
Anne Harvey and Frances Pedder were baptised
in this parish, on a personal profession of Faith
April 22nd 1791 and became the founders of the
Baptist Church in this place
'Peace to their memory'

Thomas Harvey, Ann's husband, made his will in 1798, and Ann was admitted to the lands in which she had a life interest the following year. She lived just long enough to be included as a householder living in Millgate in the

1821 census. John Pedder, the surviving executor of Thomas Harvey's will, sold the estate to Robert Harvey in 1823. The abstract of title does not mention Robert's relationship to Ann and Thomas. We think he was probably their son, although as a carver and gilder, he had chosen not to follow his father's occupation of millwright. In time Robert, too, became a pillar of the Baptist church, and his epitaph records his death in 1842:

For 50 years he was a zealous and devoted Christian
The last 12 of which he sustained the Deacon's office
in the church assembling in this place.
He rests from his Labours
and his works do follow him.

Robert's will is interesting, as it provides further evidence of family relationships. He left the property (excluding Maiden's Bower, which he had sold to Francis Parmeter in 1825) to his sister, Ann Harvey, for her life, and then to his other sister, Catherine Bane, wife of John Bane, 'Dissenting Minister'. After both sisters had died, the estate was to go to one of his executors, John Pedder Bane, millwright. The other executor was John Bane, and in 1846 we find them both described as living in Downham Market.

We think the family tree looks like this:

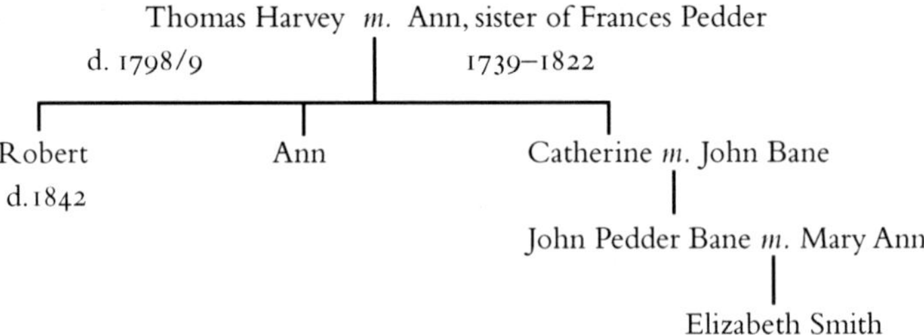

A map drawn in February 1855 (reproduced opposite) shows the property in the corner between Millgate and Mill Row, and gives the name of John Bane, presumably as trustee, as the owner. The land seems to have remained in the hands of the descendants of John Bane until 1950, when the representatives of John Pedder Bane's daughter, Mrs Elizabeth Smith, then deceased, sold it. Elizabeth had built a "villa" on the land in 1899, and this was number 46 Millgate in 1950.

MAP OF AN ESTATE IN AYLSHAM, NORFOLK.

REFERENCE

	Nos	Description	Pastures A	Pastures r	Pastures p	Houses A	Houses r	Houses p
F	1	Water Mill, Build^gs & Yards	..	..	..	.	1	5
C	2	House Build^gs Yards & Garden	..	..	.	1	2	2
C	3	House and Garden	..	..	..	.	.	24
C	4	House and Garden	..	.	.	.	.	10
C	5	House, Build^gs & Garden	..	..	..	.	2	30
C	6	Cottages and Gardens	..	.	.	.	1	19
* F	7	Malt House, Stable &c	..	.	.	.	1	37
C	8	Pond Meadow	1	2	11	..	..	..
C	9	Cascade Meadow	.	2	5	..	..	..
F	10	Dam Meadow	.	2	14	..	..	..
L	11	Granary and Staithe	.	.	.	.	1	6
C	12	Cinder Oven and Yard ..	.	.	.	.	1	6
C	13	Pool Meadow	1	3	16	.	.	.
C	14	Cottages and Gardens	.	.	.	.	.	21
C	15	Warehouses and Staithe	1	2	34	.	.	.
			6	1	3	4	.	.
		Pasture	..	..	..	6	1	3
		Total ...				10	1	9

*C Y^e Ladder Room adjoining number 7 and included in the measurement thereof } . . . . . .

3 CHAINS TO AN INCH

John Fielde

John Fielde was born about 1762, probably in Saxthorpe. He was listed twice in 1821 in the rough notebook of William Morris, the Aylsham census enumerator. He occupied a house in Millgate with two women, presumably his wife, Ann, and his daughter, also called Ann. In addition, his name appears as the owner of three houses being built either in Workhouse Pightle, or 'against Mr Rackham's'.

His first appearance in the Millgate Papers dates from 1820, and describes him as a millwright. A sale notice advertises two small pieces of land west of the road leading from Aylsham to Ingworth; one containing 20 perches and owned by Samuel and Ann Bircham and Robert Parmeter, and the other, of three acres and 35 perches, owned by Thomas and Elizabeth Francis. On 17th October 1820 John Fielde was admitted to these copyhold lands at the court of the Manor of Aylsham Lancaster. He followed this up in 1823 by buying a strip of land 27 feet by ten feet, in the same area, from John and Mary Warden.

His acquisitions were by no means confined to land west of the Cromer road. In the ten years from 1821 to 1831 he bought four properties in the Millgate area, all copyhold of the Manor of Aylsham Wood. In 1821 he paid Thomas Rackham and his daughter, Hannah, £427 for a messuage in Millgate 'wherein John Mash lately did, and John Fielde now, lives, with outhouses, yard, garden and orchard' (presumably the property mentioned in the census, and already occupied by the Fieldes), and for two acres, one rood and 22 perches of arable land to the west of the house, and for a meadow of two acres and 33 perches north of the arable field (Wright's map 330–333; 337–339?). In 1829 he added a strip of land 75 yards in length and nine yards wide, south of Robert Parmeter's malthouse, for which he paid Robert Parmeter £145 (Wright's map 329).

His other purchases in the Manor of Aylsham Wood were of land north of the River Bure. In 1830 he bought from the executors of the late John Steward two pieces of copyhold land containing together six acres, three roods and 30 perches between Tuttington Road on the south and the road 'leading from the North Walsham road into the said Tuttington road on the east part' [Wright's map 391, 390 and 389?]. These lands were part of a holding of ten acres which John Tuck surrendered for £350 in 1817 to John

Steward, defined 'by an ancient description': five acres adjacent to Kirkhill Moor on the west, two acres called Bundalls abutting upon Kirkhill Moor on the east, another property not named, and three acres called Kirkhill (Wright's map 391, 390 and 389?). The last purchase by John Fielde of which we have record, was of four acres, one rood and 22 perches bought from James Hunt Holley in 1831 'to the use of Anne Fielde' (Wright's map 387).

John Fielde made his will in that year. He left all his property in Aylsham to his wife Ann for her life, and then to his daughter, Ann. His executors were Robert William Parmeter, Gentleman, of Aylsham, and William Hase, ironfounder, of Saxthorpe, and he left £30 to each of them for their trouble. The property he left in his will was valued at under £5,000. He left all his property in Saxthorpe to his daughter, Ann. In addition, he left £500 to be 'safely invested' to provide income for his wife, and a further £1,000 to be invested to provide income for his daughter. It looks as though John Fielde may have married a Miss Hase of Saxthorpe, and that this may explain in part his ability to accumulate his land holdings.

He died in 1837, and Mrs and Miss Fielde were admitted by the Aylsham Lancaster Manor Court to the property west of the Ingworth road. In 1839, Ann, his daughter, now Mrs Phillippo, wife of Matthias Phillippo, surgeon of Norwich, was admitted to the copyhold property that her father had held of the Manor of Aylsham Wood, 'expectant on the decease . . . of her mother'.

Mrs Fielde died in 1847, and Ann Phillippo in 1868 or 1869. Ann's daughter, Ann Elizabeth Aldis of Eaton, Norwich, was admitted to all the land her grandfather had held in both Manors. After she died in 1905 the whole estate was sold to John Flaxman Daniels, an Aylsham farmer, by John Brown Aldis, widower, and his three children, all trustees under Ann Elizabeth's will. So the estate put together by John Fielde passed out of the hands of his descendants.

The Wright family

A study of the census returns from 1841 to 1881 reveals a number of men named Wright whose occupations were associated with the river, either as watermen, boatwrights or boatbuilders. Since our study is of the Millgate area only, some of the Wrights disappear after only one entry; they may have moved to other parts of Aylsham, Norfolk, or further afield.

The best-known family of Wrights is that of the boatwright and boatbuilding family, starting with Thomas Wright, boatbuilder, listed in the Riches directory of 1843. An 1850 directory lists Robert and Thomas Wright, boatbuilders, and *Kelly's Directory* of 1883 lists Elijah Wright, boatbuilder of Millgate. There are also another large number of Wrights belonging to the family of Bartlett Wright, waterman.

Boatwrights and boatbuilders

In the census of 1841, Thomas Wright, aged 50, a boatbuilder, of the Staithe, is listed with his wife Mary and children Elizabeth (15) and James (12). It is quite possible they had older children who had moved from the family home. Robert Wright (35), boatwright, living on the west side of Millgate, is listed with his wife Elizabeth and five children.

The census of 1851, which gives more complete details, shows that Robert and Elizabeth have a further three children, and the older two have moved out. The full list of the children's names is: Elizabeth, Robert, Mary, David, James, Annie, Harriet and Elijah. There is also a reference in the parish churchyard survey to two children who died in infancy – Thomas and Hannah.

Thomas Wright, boatbuilder, did not feature in the Millgate area in 1851. However, Geoffrey Nobbs in his article 'Aylsham river in the last century' refers to Thomas Wright, master boatbuilder, aged 62, as being listed in the 1851 census. There is also a Thomas Wright, waterman, aged 28 and married to Anne. He may be the son of Thomas Wright, boatbuilder. He was not listed in later census returns, but could be the Thomas Wright recorded as landlord of the Anchor Inn between 1868 and 1872 and also water bailiff during the same period.

By the 1871 census, Robert's three sons David, James and Elijah have moved from the family home, and live with their wives in Millgate. They are listed as boatwrights (in 1861 as boat builders). There are no Thomases listed. The 1881 census does not list any of Robert's sons, only his daughter, Harriet Neale, living in Millgate with her husband. Robert has obviously died. A later Kelly's directory of 1883 lists Elijah Wright, boatbuilder, of Millgate. He was the youngest son of Robert, and perhaps had the advantage of being the only one there when his father became elderly. After looking at details of the Aylsham population prepared for the 1821 census, it would seem very likely that Thomas and Robert were both sons of Thomas Wright of Millgate 'towards the Mill', employed in trade.

Watermen

There was a Bartlett Wright in 1821 living in Millgate, listed as having two sons, and not being in trade. A second Bartlett Wright, waterman, living in Millgate, is noted in the census of 1851. He is absent, but his young wife Harriet, aged 19, and his son Bartlett are present. In 1861, Bartlett Wright is described as 'waterman – master rivercraft'; his son, aged 12, is a waterman's assistant, and there are three more sons, Thomas, William and Frederick and baby Harriet. By 1881, Harriet Wright is a widow, charwoman, living in Mill Row, having had three more children. Her son, James (16) is described as a waterman. Frederick had been described as an agricultural labourer.

It is conceivable that the Bartlett Wright listed in 1821 is a younger brother of Thomas and Robert, and became a waterman because there was no room in the family business of boatbuilding, or because he preferred the mobile life on the river. Robert made sure that each of his sons had the skill of boatwright. His daughters married watermen or bricklayers.

It is recorded that Bob Wright built racing boats for the Aylsham Regatta in the mid-nineteenth century. In the leaflet prepared by the Norfolk Museums Service we read that

> *The boatyards of Thomas and Robert Wright in the first half of the 19th century, and Elijah Wright in the second half, had achieved great distinction. One Aylsham-built wherry, named the Gypsy, had been sailed by her owner, Henry Doughty, on all the waterways of Europe, and her travels were recorded in his books.*

Bob Wright's son, David, then aged 34, a boatwright, and married, is last noted in Millgate in 1871. He lived very near to his widowed father. One may conjecture that the forecast coming of the railways made young men adapt their skills and move from the river in the last part of the nineteenth century

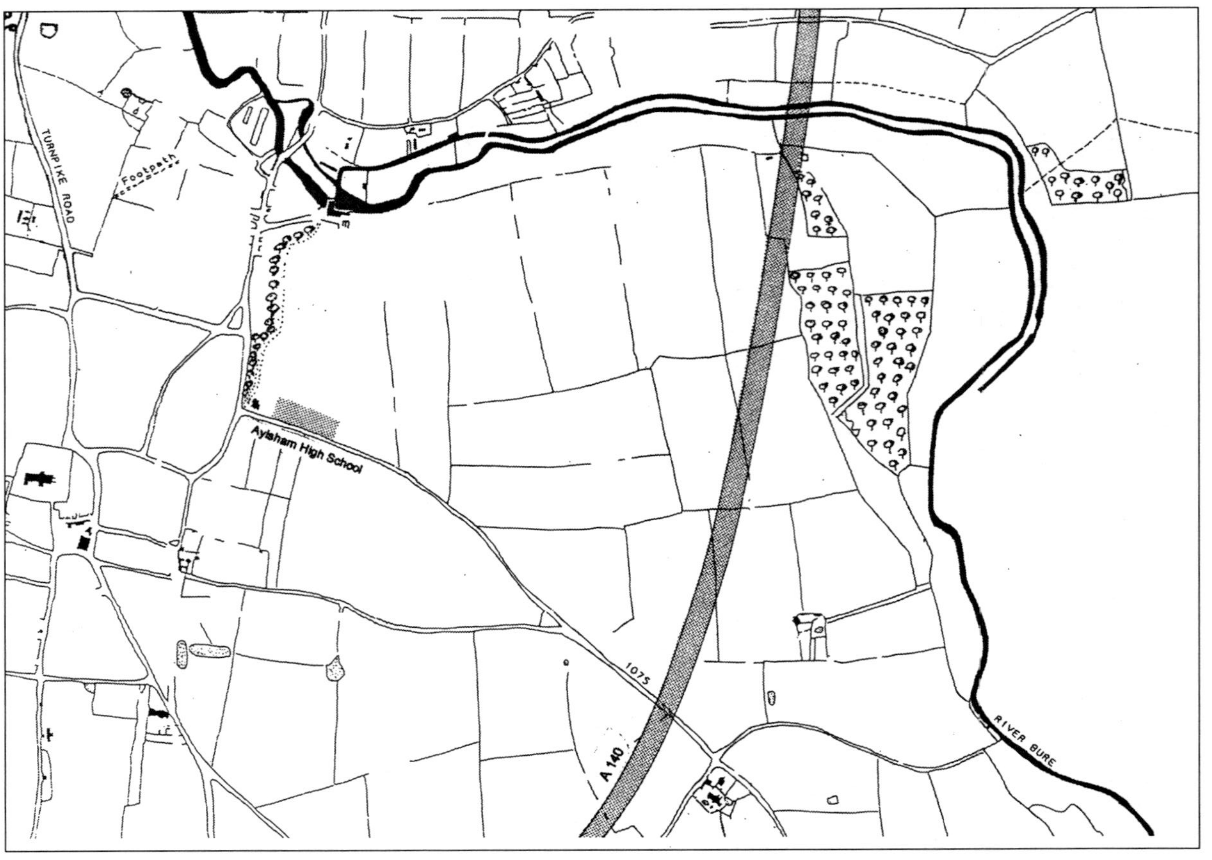

Map showing the Belt estate with the position of the present High School and bypass superimposed.

9

The Wickes family and the Belt estate

At the end of Mill Row, just past the Aylsham water mill, lie the remains of the Belt estate and the farm house which is now known simply as the Belt. The house has now become one of those grand secret houses which still exist in country towns like Aylsham. Today it is first seen from the back with its Italianate series of arched colonnades, facing the remains of a small formal garden separated from the river Bure by a high brick wall. On the other side of the house the more formal Georgian front is an unexpected surprise to a visitor. When the house was the centre of the estate it was approached by a long drive from a small thatched lodge at the corner of Williams Lane and Gay's Lane (now Sir William's Lane and Gas House Hill). The drive ran down the hill beside a wood which skirted the backs of houses on Millgate Street and near to the bottom made a right turn up to the house front. The lodge has changed over the last hundred years, and was originally a small building. It has been extended to nearly twice its size, re-thatched and is now completely separated from the estate, the drive and its original function.

The story of the family which amassed this estate and the farm house had its own secrets and curiosities which will become clear as the story of the Wickes family unfolds. It is also the story of the demise of two of the Norfolk families who owned the Belt. There were no male heirs to carry

The Belt Lodge, the entrance to the Belt estate at the corner of Sir William's Lane and Gas House Hill.

the name and inherit the estate, either for the Wickes family or for that branch of the Kerrison family which owned the house for some years before the story reaches the present day.

The history of the Wickes family begins in the early 1700s when Samuel Clarke, a prosperous grocer in Aylsham, married Elizabeth Langwade. Soon after their marriage he bought a property known as 'Paradise', an L-shaped piece of ground and house just behind St Michael's church. They appear to have lived there for the rest of their lives and it was in 'Paradise' that their daughter Ruth and their other children were born. The great-grandfather of Samuel Clarke was a woollen draper from Scarning, but the Clarke children and their descendants had spread out across Norfolk to Norwich, Wymondham, Hethersett and Skeyton. Samuel and Elizabeth Clarke were both born in Skeyton and were eventually buried there, but during their busy life in Aylsham they had five children, although three died in infancy. In 1794 the eldest daughter Ruth married John Wickes, a successful tanner from Blickling.

How successful his tanning business was is difficult to determine, although there was a vast increase in the use of leather throughout the country. During the period when horses were the power source in agriculture it was used for harnesses, saddles, carriage springs and leather covering for carriages. Domestically it was in use as wall hangings, leather clothes and footwear and in industry for straps and belting. Blickling and the surrounding countryside may not have generated a substantial need for leather, but Norwich and other cities became centres of distribution throughout the country. Even at that time imported hides, being cheaper, began to undercut the home market and inevitably the industry slowly declined in size. However, John Wickes seems to have moved up the Aylsham social ladder as a result of his business ability, but it is not clear if the business was moved from Blickling or if he simply started another tannery in Aylsham. In time his son and grandchildren were also listed as tanners in the local directories, and Wright's survey of 1839 simply records that they owned a tan yard near the Belt house, very close to the river.

John and Ruth Wickes had two boys, the elder, Rice Wickes, eventually moving to Eaton on the edge of Norwich while his younger brother William Wickes stayed in Aylsham. Rice Wickes remained single all his life, eventually inheriting his grandfather's property 'Paradise', and that inheritance seems to have brought him back into Aylsham. In 1811 the younger brother, William, married Susanna from Crostwick and they had four children, William Watts, Ellen, Susan E. and another Rice Wickes. In October 1814 they bought a large stretch of land for £9,800 from Benjamin and Sarah Walker. Susanna seems to have been involved in the running of their business from the beginning and it could well have been a joint decision to buy from the Walkers. This large acquisition formed the beginning of the Belt estate and the price they were able to pay for the land indicates the success of their tanning business. It is interesting to contrast this figure with the wage of an agricultural worker whose wage at that time was 12 shillings a week. Because of an agricultural slump six years later, wages dropped to ten shillings a week and then to eight shillings.

The forename 'Rice' was not uncommon at the time, but in this family it was short lived, since the nephew died when he was 22, and had little time to pass it on, and his uncle had no such intention. William as a first name was used by three generations of Wickes beginning with John Wickes whose father may also have been William, and then going down through his children and grandchildren. Susan Ellen the youngest daughter is little more than a name; she lived in the shadow of her mother, and was her companion for the rest of her mother's life until the mother died in 1857. Her sister Ellen however married Rev. William Wayte Andrew from Gimingham, who later became the vicar at Ketteringham. His proposal was typical of the man. He first asked her mother if she was engaged, then declared: 'I am convinced that it is for God's glory that I should become a married man. I have made it a subject of earnest prayer and I seem to have been directed to your house. I shall therefore consider your answer the answer of God.' Both parents were devout churchgoers and could only agree; the couple were married at Aylsham on 18th March 1834. The following January the first of their six surviving children was born, a son who was baptised William Wickes Andrew and eventually became a barrister. However, the vicar and his wife were a quarrelsome couple; William Andrew took offence easily; any perceived slight to his beliefs or his position in society made that person an enemy – a state which, once achieved, was almost impossible to shed. The local squire, Sir John Boileau, unknowingly offended Mr Andrew, before they met, by purchasing a house that Andrew had hoped to buy. Their relationship was always fractious and after this slight the difficulties were increased by their position in the local society. Vanity was to play a large part in their differences, each assumed social rights which were attached to their different positions as a squire and this clergyman whom he was unable to discharge. Mrs Ellen Andrew could be equally difficult, although most of her disagreements were on behalf of her husband, and she had a series of quarrels with the squire which she conducted quite independently of her husband. The story of the Andrews and their various disagreements and difficulties is told in *Victorian Miniature* by Owen Chadwick.

The oldest of William and Susanna's four children was certainly the most interesting. William Watts Wickes was married in 1835 to Ellen, who came from Burgate in Suffolk. He was listed as a tanner in the local directories and presumably had joined his father's business as a tanner. William and his son William Watts lived at the Belt with their families as well as the sister Susan E. while their uncle, Rice Wickes, lived in a 'neat mansion' in Aylsham. In 1835 William Wickes died and two years later William Watts Wickes inherited the whole of his father's estate. William Watts and his wife Ellen continued to live at the Belt house, but so did his mother Susanna and his sister Susan. Soon after the estate had been settled, William Watts Wickes left the Belt estate and went to live 40 miles away in Thetford where he established himself as a Wine and Spirit Merchant and Brewer.

It is unclear when or why he changed his whole life in this dramatic way, but one probable explanation could revolve around his position at the Belt estate. The tanning and agricultural businesses were his father's and his mother's businesses and although he had inherited the property it was clear that his mother had not relinquished her control over it. After the death of her husband she had assumed direction over the property and remained the driving force there until she died in 1857. In addition to this assumption of power by his mother, both his sister and his wife continued to live at the Belt, but these two were beholden in their different ways to this matriarch. After the death of his father there was little to keep him in Aylsham and his move to Thetford gave him both freedom and the possibility of a new venture. He presumably took with him some of his inheritance which enabled him to establish himself quickly in this new town. It also appears he acquired a new wife in Thetford; her name was Lydia Wickes. It is unlikely they were married and probably lived together under an assumed title. Unfortunately their married life was cut short when she died in the March of 1839 aged 26 and was buried at St Peter's church in Thetford. It is possible she died in childbirth, which was not uncommon, but there are no details of her life or the nature of her death.

His new business seems to have flourished, and as a result he became an Alderman in 1845 and three years later was elected to the position of Mayor, and again in 1855. His mother's death in 1857 probably triggered his eventual return to Aylsham because in 1858 he instructed Henry Newson, a local auctioneer, to auction the Raymond Street Brewery, which included a Brewhouse, a large Tun-Room, Mill House, cellars, stabling and offices. In addition to the brewery there was an adjoining family residence, and at the rear of the brewery on the corner of Nether Row a public house called The Victorian Shades. None of these buildings survived post-war rebuilding. In addition there were eight other public houses across Norfolk and Suffolk, another maltings at Wymondham and various parcels of land. All of them were to be auctioned at the Bell Inn on 7th June 1858. The Thetford brewery, maltings and Public House were auctioned again in August 1863 and were probably bought by Bidwell & Co. Two of William Watts Wickes' fellow Aldermen, while he lived in Thetford, were father and son, Leonard Shelford Bidwell and Shelford Clarke Bidwell. A Shelford Bid-

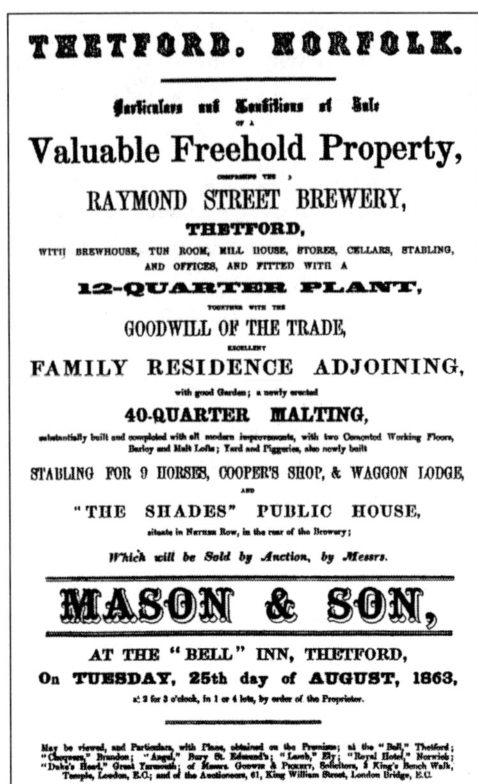

THETFORD, NORFOLK.

Particulars and Conditions of Sale

OF A

Valuable Freehold Property,

COMPRISING THE

RAYMOND STREET BREWERY,

THETFORD,

WITH BREWHOUSE, TUN ROOM, MILL HOUSE, STORES, CELLARS, STABLING, AND OFFICES, AND FITTED WITH A

12-QUARTER PLANT,

TOGETHER WITH THE

GOODWILL OF THE TRADE,

EXCELLENT

FAMILY RESIDENCE ADJOINING,

with good Garden; a newly erected

40-QUARTER MALTING,

substantially built and completed with all modern improvements, with two Cemented Working Floors, Barley and Malt Lofts; Yard and Piggeries, also newly built

STABLING FOR 9 HORSES, COOPER'S SHOP, & WAGGON LODGE,

AND

"THE SHADES" PUBLIC HOUSE,

situate in Nether Row, in the rear of the Brewery;

Which will be Sold by Auction, by Messrs.

MASON & SON,

AT THE "BELL" INN, THETFORD,

On TUESDAY, 25th day of AUGUST, 1863,

at 2 for 3 o'clock, in 1 or 4 lots, by order of the Proprietor.

May be viewed, and Particulars, with Plans, obtained on the Premises; at the "Bell," Thetford; "Chequers," Brandon; "Angel," Bury St. Edmund's; "Lamb," Ely; "Royal Hotel," Norwich; "Duke's Head," Great Yarmouth; of Messrs. Godwin & Pickett, Solicitors, 2 King's Bench Walk, Temple, London, E.C.; and of the Auctioneers, 61, King William Street, London Bridge, E.C.

well was recorded as the first in the family to brew beer in Thetford, which he did in 1795, and the family eventually became Bidwell & Co. The company bought and owned public houses across East Anglia and were also brewers, selling their beers through their own houses. Eventually they acquired the Raymond Street Brewery and the Victorian Shades, but in 1904 the whole estate of 105 hotels, public houses and beerhouses was sold.

William Watts Wickes, now free of his Thetford life and attachments, returned to Aylsham and was once again living at the Belt farm house. He was now 42 and referred to as a Landed Proprietor. His wife Ellen, two years younger, was still living at the Belt with three servants. After his return they appear to have entertained more visitors, and although in the past three servants had sufficed, they now acquired a butler. His sister, a wraith in this story, seems to have disappeared by the time he had returned to the Belt. In 1875 William Watts Wickes died; his will, which was dated 20th November 1872, had to be proved twice, once in 1875 and again in 1891. His widow Ellen Watts Wickes continued to live at the Belt until she died in 1891 aged 74. After her death the estate was managed by trustees. Her death closed this branch of the family and since there was no other Wickes waiting in discreet obscurity to administer the estate, it was sold in 1894. William Frederick Starling (1851–1937) refers in his *Memories of Aylsham* to his father who sold baskets in his shop in Red Lion Street and employed a number of basket makers. He occupied three acres of the Belt estate in the form of two enclosures, and he paid a yearly rent of £16 5*s* 0*d*. One was a

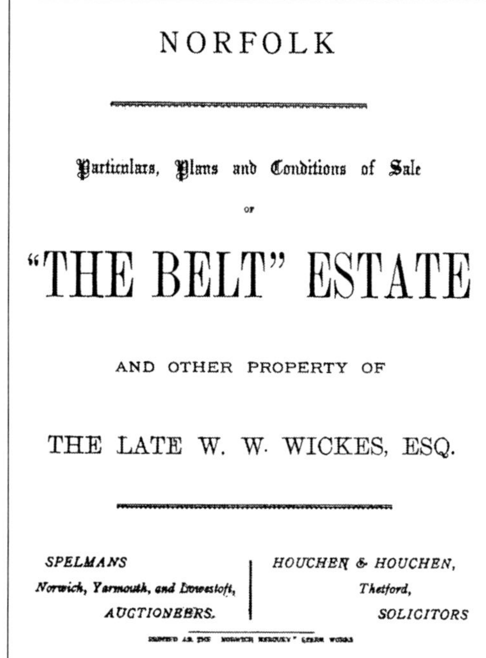

NORFOLK

Particulars, Plans and Conditions of Sale

OF

"THE BELT" ESTATE

AND OTHER PROPERTY OF

THE LATE W. W. WICKES, ESQ.

SPELMANS
Norwich, Yarmouth, and Lowestoft,
AUCTIONEERS.

HOUCHEN & HOUCHEN,
Thetford,
SOLICITORS

pasture and the other an Osier Carr close to the River Bure. The willows which were cut from this land were made into baskets by his basket makers and then sold in the Aylsham shop. When the estate was sold he lost the use of both of these pieces of land which was part of a small farm on the far side of the estate. This loss to Starling seems to have been quickly restored because his son writes that he was later growing 100 acres of osiers on rented land at Barton. As a result of the sale, the estate was eventually bought by the Kerrison family of Burgh Hall and the proceeds from the sale were divided amongst the children of Ellen Andrew.

The Belt estate was then amalgamated with other areas of land owned by the Kerrisons, or was acquired by them later, and this large estate passed through a number of generations of Kerrisons. Lieut-Col. Edmond Roger Allday Kerrison, the head of the family, had spent half his life in the army and it was not until the early part of the century that he left the army and settled at Burgh Hall. In due course the estate was taken over by his son Roger Fulke Kerrison and eventually by his grandson.

In 1878 Benjamin Cook bought the Dunkirk Roller Mill, which was across the river and the canal. He also acquired the Belt farm house which he occupied until he retired in 1907. Although both mills are on the periphery of this story, as they are with the estate, there are some interesting connections. Cook had a number of interests in the milling industry, and owned mills at Itteringham and Blickling. He made considerable technical improvements to the Dunkirk roller mill and a lot of the flour and other milled products were shipped out on wherries down the canal. The other side of Ben Cook's life is also interesting since he organised gambling parties at the Belt. Mr Cook ensured that all the gamblers at the table had a similar income, so wagers were comparable and there were no uncomfortable moments around the size of the bids occurred. He worshipped at St Michael's church and in 1890 commissioned a mission room to be built on ground adjoining the churchyard at a cost of £400; the building still stands and was used for a time as a Parish room. He married a much younger woman quite late in life and died in 1913. Mrs Cook, who had married when she was 26, remained a widow until 1970 when she died aged 89.

After the Cooks had left the Belt it was occupied by a number of tenants, some of whom worked for the mills, but it was not until 1916 that the Belt was occupied for a continuous period by just a few tenants. A retired army Major, Harold Herbert Johnson, stayed there until 1922 and then moved to the Knoll in the Blickling Road. He was followed by Herbert Berty Neave and his wife. Neave was a farmer who remained at the Belt until 1929 and farmed in the area until they moved to Abbots House. In 1932 the Kerrisons sold the Belt and some of the estate to the Holmans. The Holmans built a bungalow in the grounds for their own use, but during the war the Belt was used to house evacuee school children from London, and also landgirls, although not at the same time.

In 1954 the Kerrisons sold off the field beside Sir William's Lane on the edge of the Belt estate, which provided an area of land where the High School could be built. At the time of the opening a number of trees were planted in the school grounds spelling the name Aylsham. During the hurricane of 1987 some of the trees were damaged and then later replaced. The Belt house was sold in 1999, and a few years later resold and has now been restored by its present owners as a private house. Little now remains of the original estate; the canal which ran parallel to the River Bure and had been an important industrial waterway was destroyed in the flood of 1912. Both the canal and the river, which had defined two sides of the estate, have declined into two wide ditches running under the A140 bypass. The Aylsham bypass, which was opened in 1980, divides a large section of what had been the Belt estate. The Wickes family has now died out and the Kerrisons who inherited the estate are now represented by two sisters. With the break-up and decline of the Belt estate a large colourful part of Aylsham's history has now, like the River Bure, meandered into the past.

10

Searching for the New Jerusalem

Although several of the Millgate personalities were referred to in earlier chapters there are others who require a chapter to themselves. These are the people whose lives were so closely interconnected that they need to be considered as a group. One such group is that of the Power, Berry and Clover families.

On the east side of Millgate, and south of Mill Row, is a group of small properties which are an interesting example of how, over a period of 150 years, the use of a site develops and changes in different hands. They also show how Millgate inhabitants were an integral part of the town, owning property and working in other areas, and contributing to its social and religious life. The properties are the present numbers 28-34 Millgate; the Stonemason's Arms; and numbers 42 and 44 Millgate (Wright's map schedule nos 305 and 306).

Our information starts with the marriage in 1743 of a John Power, farmer of Alby and 'barber surgeon of Aylsham', to Ann Drosier of Banningham. She was the daughter of Edward Drosier, a tanner. They had three children: John, Mary and Ann. They planned to divide their properties (some of which were in other parts of Aylsham as well as Millgate) between the three children, but in the event only Mary survived her parents, and as Mary Berry, widow of John Berry who had been Master of the Bridewell, she inherited all her parents' possessions in 1789. Their property in Millgate was described as two roods of land on which was one tenement and, later, two tenements or cottages, and adjoining pightle.

In 1820, Mary Berry died leaving all her property to the artist Joseph Clover. He, in his turn, had inherited property in Millgate from his father, but by this time he was not living there. It is interesting to speculate on why she did this, and we will come back to this later. Around 1840, Joseph Clover sold all his Millgate properties to John Freeman, who was a stonemason and already resident in Millgate – the bond describes the transaction as 'a bond for the quiet enjoyment of the property'. Later, through a mortgage indenture of 1863, we find that John Freeman has had built, on the pightle of land, a public house with a stonemason's yard, outbuildings, yards and gardens. He also still held the two adjacent tenements previously described. His daughters later inherited and bought half each. Fanny Freeman, who later married Richard Chapman, paid £900 for four cottages (which had replaced the earlier two tenements) i.e. Nos. 28–34, the stonemason's yard, and the Stonemason's Arms, which by then had been let to Messrs Bullard & Co. Her sister, married to Edmund Balls, executor of the property, retained land to the north and at some point they must have built Nos 42 and 44. Richard Chapman and his children inherited the property, and when he died in 1926 the property (by this time one shop, three cottages and the stonemason's yard) was sold. Copies of the sale notices still exist. The properties were bought individually by Messrs Pert, Dyball and Atkins. We do not know when the inn was sold.

Now to come back to Mary Berry and her bequest to Joseph Clover the artist. So far, our information has come from deeds in the 'Bishop bundles'. Other sources, including Clover family papers, have helped us to find possible reasons for her bequest and have drawn our attention to certain happenings in the religious life of Aylsham.

The Clover family were well known in Aylsham and in Norwich. (Their frequent use of the Christian names Joseph and Thomas makes for identification problems at times.) Thomas Clover, son of a well-known Norwich farrier and veterinary surgeon, came to Aylsham, became a shopkeeper, married an Ann Barnard and lived in Millgate. This family were neighbours and, it would seem, close friends of the Power family. It was this family friendship, lasting over many years and spanning more than one generation, which probably lay behind the bequest. Thomas and Ann had a large family, most of whom died young and are buried in the grave close by the charnel house in the churchyard. Three sons grew into adult life; one was Joseph, the artist (1779–1853), who trained as an engraver and then became a portrait painter of some distinction, studying under Opie in London. He also exhibited at the annual exhibitions of the Norwich Society of Artists, founded by John Crome, and also, later, at the Royal Academy. He was betrothed to Mary Berry's daughter Ann, who died in 1801, aged 20. He remained a bachelor all his life.

The second son was John Wright Clover (1780–1865), who in 1803 took over the family business on the corner of the Market Place and Hungate Street. He married twice; the first was a runaway marriage to Gretna Green with Elizabeth Taylor, the daughter of a Harleston clergyman. She died aged 28, leaving a daughter, Ann. He later married (more advantageously perhaps) the niece of John Bayfield Peterson – Elizabeth Mary Ann Peterson, who inherited Abbots Hall (known at that time as Aylsham Wood House). They had a number of children, the most eminent of whom was the pioneer anaesthetist Joseph Clover, recently commemorated by a plaque on the wall of the new King Chemist building on the site of the former Clover shop in the Market Place. The third son was Thomas (1781–?), a farmer in Colby, who married Maria Cook in 1804 and had a number of children.

The other link between these two families was a religious one, and came to light when, in the course of investigating the extent and whereabouts of Mary Berry's property in the town, it was discovered that in 1796 she had bought a Meeting House. From the Clover family papers, from letters and other records, it is clear that the Meeting House was to be used as a New Jerusalem Church according to the beliefs of a religious group called Swedenborgians. This sect are followers of Emanuel Swedenborg who was a Swedish scientist and writer during the eighteenth century. The writings of Emanuel Swedenborg seem to have attracted interest amongst artists and literary figures including William Blake (for a short time only), John Flaxman, Elizabeth Barrett Browning and Helen Keller. The congregations were called the New Jerusalem Church, and clergy and ministers from different denominations were involved in starting them in different parts of the country. John Wright Clover was closely involved in Aylsham and Joseph Clover was closely associated with the London church, and was a trustee from 1822 to 1826. From other sources, it would seem that his father, and probably an uncle in Norwich, were associated with the starting of the Norwich church in 1801.

Where was this Meeting House? A bond of 1796, recording the transaction between Mary Berry and a John Boardman, reads:

> *All that new erected Meeting House situate in Aylsham including seats, pews and other features now standing and being therein, and also all that cottage or West End of a tenement situate in Aylsham aforesaid, near the said Meeting House, and now in the occupation of William Shreeve; and also all those pieces and parcels of land adjoining and belonging to the said premises, or to some part thereof.*

Her daughter Ann (died 1801), Thomas Wright Clover (died 1803) and Dr Saunders, an Aylsham surgeon, became trustees. From the Aylsham Lancaster Manor Court Books we know that the building was in existence in 1791, having been erected on land belonging to a Richard Jex and his wife, and surrendered by him to John Boardman of Gorleston, from whom it passed into the possession of Mary Berry. The Manor Court Rolls describe in detail the 'pieces and parcels of land' mentioned in the bond. They include a cottage and a long passage way next to the east end of the cottage leading from a gateway from the street on the north to the Meeting House. The description of the Meeting House and land closely resembles the present Baptist church and its situation, and its description in the Baptist Bicentenary Booklet of 1991. Recent measurements have confirmed that the oldest part of the present Baptist Church must have been the Meeting House bought by Mary Berry.

There are certain other significant dates, facts and events which make interesting reading, and create a picture of the life of the various dissenting communities in Aylsham which is at once confusing and intriguing and needs interpreting. In 1789, we learn from the Dissenter Meeting Houses register that a Richard Jex was licensed to hold dissenters' meetings on his premises, described as a 'former combing house' converted into a schoolroom. By 1791, we know that the new Meeting House had been erected.

Methodist tradition has it that it was built by the Methodists, and licensed in the name of Rev. Thomas Tattersall of Norwich, named in Charles Wesley's records. By 1842, they had sold it to the Baptists, having built the new Methodist Chapel on the roadside in White Hart Street. The Aylsham Baptists' Bicentenary Booklet notes that Rev. Joseph Kinghorn, from Norwich, started the Baptist Church in Aylsham by the baptism of five believers in the River Bure in April 1791. Mention is made in a Norwich Baptist Minute Book of members going to Aylsham in 1787. They believe that the Meeting House was built by a Baptist speculative builder called Wilks, and that he allowed Rev. Joseph Kinghorn to use it. Maybe he allowed the Methodists to use it, too, or vice versa?

We know from Browne's *History of Congregationalism* that in 1791 Rev. Samuel Crowther from Clare in Suffolk was ordained minister of the Independent (Congregational) Chapel or Meeting House in Oulton. He is known to have preached in Aylsham on a number of occasions, and to have formed a congregation there which, after a short time, combined with the congregation in Oulton. We know also that he was married a year or two later to a Mary Boardman and, some years later still, to a Susannah Boardman.

In 1791, as noted above, possession of the Meeting House, according to Manor Court Rolls, passed from Richard Jex to John Boardman of Gorleston.

The next significant date seems to be 1796, when Mary Berry purchased the Meeting House from John Boardman (whose interest and role in all this is so far not known – he may have had Baptist interests). Her interest, however, is very clear. There exist two letters written by Mrs Berry, one to a Mr Clover (presumably J.W.) in 1798, and another (not addressed) in 1804, showing her commitment to the New Jerusalem Church. She covenants to surrender the church to its trustees, and expressly states that she wishes to ensure that no one should be expected to contribute financially to its upkeep unless they can afford to do so. She wants to arrange instruction for two poor children of parents interested in the New Church (to be chosen by Mr Clover), and she is prepared to make books available for their instruction, which could later be passed on to other deserving children. She refers, in the earlier letter, to a Mr Crowther as the person she expects may undertake the teaching. Was he the same Mr Crowther as the minister at Oulton?

In the same year, Rev. Joseph Kinghorn is said to have applied to the Baptist Fund for financial assistance, but it is not clear if he got it. He was granted possession of the land and building in 1811 by the Norwich courts as a result of disturbances against nonconformists in the town.

The picture that emerges is one of much activity in a number of nonconformist groups in the town at the end of the eighteenth century. Perhaps more than one was allowed to use the Meeting House, the first to be purpose built in the town, as opposed to meeting in private houses under licence, a practice which continued until well into the nineteenth century. Deeds and Court Rolls show who owns a property, but do not necessarily tell us which denomination they represent. Perhaps, too, the denominations were not as distinct or as separate as we tend to think of them now. There is reference in the Clover papers to the fact that 'J. W.' and his wife continue to attend the parish church, and we know that Mary Berry was buried in the churchyard of St Michael's. We do not yet know when the New Jerusalem Church in Aylsham ceased to meet.

Stone House, looking down Millgate

11

Mash's Row and the Mash family

In 1845, William Mash built a row of six red brick and flint cottages, which were known as Mash's Row, on land at the end of Millgate, near to the River Bure and Drabblegate. This area of land is referred to as Cascade Meadow, no. 529 on Wright's 1839 map schedule. A plaque with 'Freehold W.E.M. 1845' is attached to the back wall of one of the cottages, and the initials are those of William and his wife, Elizabeth Hayne Mash.

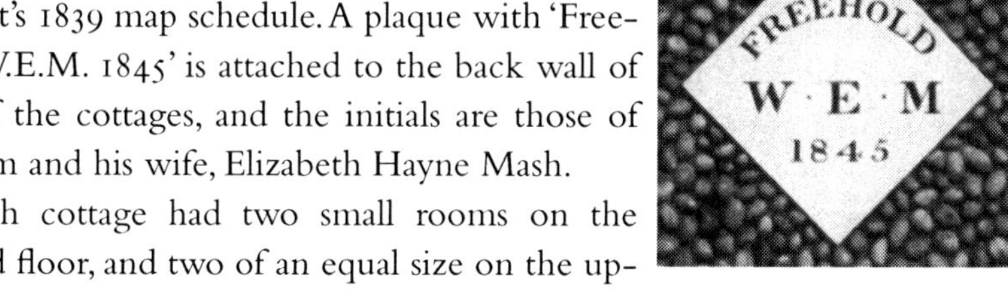

Each cottage had two small rooms on the ground floor, and two of an equal size on the upper floor, with a staircase connecting both floors. There were no bathrooms, and water for domestic purposes was drawn from a well. At the rear of each cottage there was a garden which extended to the banks of an outlet from the River Bure and, on the other side of the lane, another garden which was used for growing vegetables and soft fruit. Each cottage had a lavatory closet at the rear of the garden. The well which served the cottages was situated near to the lane in the garden of 4 Mash's Row.

Three years later, William Mash had a house built on the Millgate street side of the same piece of land. Rumour has it that the house was originally built as a public house, but never used as such, and was occupied as

one private dwelling, and subsequently converted into two semi-detached houses. The original house was square, two storeys high, with a front façade of red bricks and grey sea coast flints, in the center of which, between the two halves of the building in small cream coloured stones, are the initials W.E.M. and the date 1848. Each house has a door with a plain portico, placed at the end of the building, and two rectangular sash windows with small panes of glass, near the centre. Both sides of the original building reflected the front façade, but the back wall of the house was constructed from red bricks and large coarse flints. There is no doubt that the front appearance of the building was of greater importance than the back.

The original layout of the rooms in the house is now difficult to define, since the conversion to two separate houses, but it would appear to have had four rooms downstairs, with access through a doorway between the two front rooms. This arrangement was duplicated on the floor above. At the time of conversion, the door on the ground floor was removed and the space filled in. On the upper floor, a brick wall was built on one side in the first house, leaving the door and frame still in position on the other side. A staircase linked both floors, and a new staircase was put in at the time of conversion. There was also another small staircase in the second house, which led to a small windowless room in the loft.

In common with houses of this period, there was no bathroom, water came from a well and there was an outside closet. Both houses had front and rear gardens, and each one had a further garden on the far side of Mash's Row. The houses were deemed to be in Millgate until the 1980s when they were officially classified as numbers 1 and 2 Mash's Row, and the cottages 3–8 Mash's Row.

In the nineteenth century a one-storey brick extension with a sloping pantile roof was built on to the side of Number 2 Mash's Row. In 1914, the tenant was a Mr J. Tight, a fishmonger, who had a small smokehouse at the

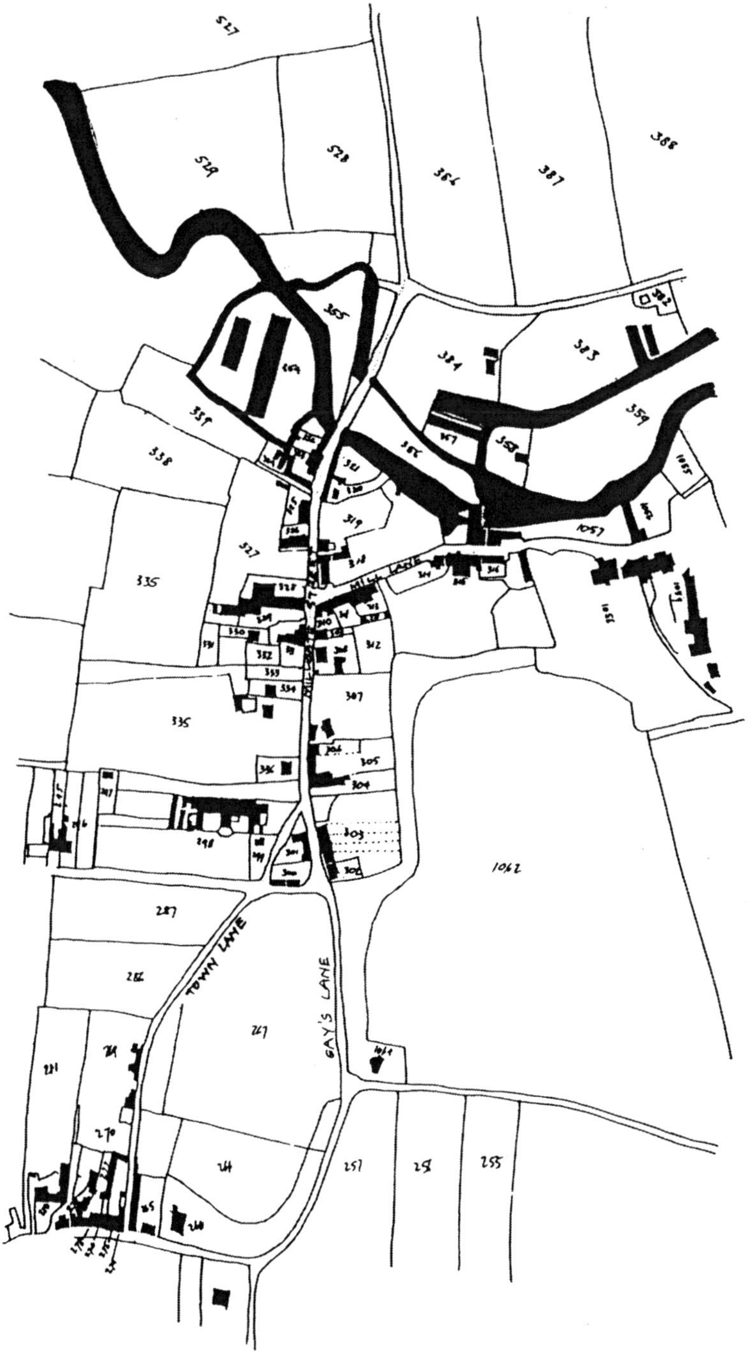

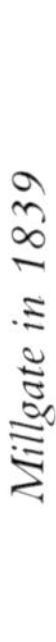

Millgate in 1839

end of the rear garden and sold fish from the front part of the extension. In 1952, this extension was altered to the full height of the house, almost doubling it in size. The secondary front door was removed in the process, a large window was inserted and the front wall was made to match the original. A small brick lean-to had been added to the rear of No. 1, which was used as a kitchen, but this was demolished in 1978 and a two-storey extension built at the rear of the house. The side wall of this extension was made to match the original. When the foundations for this extension were being dug, a well, which had been bricked over, was discovered a few yards from the back of the original building. This well had been used when the house was first occupied, and had subsequently been filled in and forgotten.

A long, low building, 50 feet by 12 feet, with an earth floor had been built at the rear of 2 Mash's Row, and it is rumoured that it was intended as a skittle alley for the public house. It was first described as a cart shed and stable, and later referred to as a barn. The barn remained in its original form until 1965 when part of it was taken down to make a conservatory and a concrete floor laid in this area, but it was not until 1991 that all the earth floor in the barn was concreted.

At the Staithe, and near to No. 1 Mash's Row, there was a small blacksmith's forge. James Martin is on record as being the blacksmith in 1858, and living in the house with his family. By 1879, John Martin and his son are listed as blacksmiths with a further forge at Burgh. John Martin was succeeded by his son, Walter John Martin, both at the Staithe and at Burgh in 1892. During the 1914–18 war troops were billeted near to the mill, and the military horses were shod by a blacksmith at the Staithe. The forge was abandoned between the wars and fell into disrepair, and was rebuilt as a double garage in the 1970s.

William Mash died in 1849. The houses and cottages in Mash's Row passed to his wife, Elizabeth Hayne Mash, and then in 1874 to their son, Henry Brett Mash. He left Mash's Row to his sister, Katherine Howlett, for her lifetime, and on her death in 1914 all the property was auctioned including the houses and cottages in Mash's Row. Ownership of Mash's Row passed out of the hands of the Mash family at this time. The auction was held at the Black Boys in Aylsham on 28th July 1914. Charles Henry Rooke, a retired innkeeper of Drabblegate, bought 1 and 2 Mash's Row as a double dwelling house with stable, cartshed, outbuildings, yards and gardens. The

S. W. BRUCE.

AYLSHAM.

STANLEY W. BRUCE is favoured with instructions from the Executor of the Will of the late Mr. Henry Brett Mash, to Sell by Public Auction, at the Black Boys Hotel, Aylsham, on TUESDAY, the 28th JULY, 1914, at Four o'clock in the Afternoon, precisely, the following valuable

FREEHOLD PROPERTY

In Aylsham, in the undermentioned or such other Lots as may be determined upon at the Sale, namely :—

Lot 1. All those Six well-built BRICK and STONE COTTAGES, with out-houses and gardens, in Millgate Street, on Gas House Hill, in the occupation of Mr. King and others at gross rentals of £32 15s. per annum.

Lot 2. All those Three well-built BRICK and STONE COTTAGES, with outhouses and gardens, in Millgate Street, adjoining Lot 1, in the occupation of Mr. Randell and others, at gross rentals of £15 12s. per annum. There is a well of good water for the above nine cottages.

Lot 3. All that substantially built DWELLING-HOUSE now known as "-STONE HOUSE," containing 6 Bedrooms, 4 Lower Rooms, Cellar, and Wash House, with a very good Garden, also Pump for hard and soft water, in Millgate Street, Gas House Hill, in the occupation of Mrs. Braithwaite, at a rental of £15 per annum.

Lot 4. All those Two conveniently built BRICK and STONE MESSUAGES with Gardens and Outbuildings, comprising Stable, and Cart Shed, in Millgate Street, facing the Midland and Great Northern Railway, now or lately occupied by Mr. J. Tight and Mrs. Martin, at a gross rental of £16 per annum.

Lot 5. All those Six well-built BRICK and STONE MESSUAGES with Out-houses and Gardens now known as "Mash's Row," with Small Piece of Land (about 0a. 1r. 14p.), near thereto, and used as a drying ground, in Millgate Street, in the occupation of Mr. R. Pratt and others, at gross rentals of £31 10s. per annum. There is a pump with a good supply of water, for Lots 4 and 5.

For Further Particulars, apply to the Auctioneer, Bank Street, Aylsham, or to

MR. C. ERNEST JACKSON,
Solicitor,
The Crescent, Wisbech

tenants at the time were Mr Tight and Mr Matthews. The six cottages were bought by a Mr Frank Searle.

The tenants living in Mash's Row in the second part of the nineteenth century had a variety of occupations – agricultural labourer, coal porter, journeyman miller, dressmaker, boat riveter, harness maker, labourer at the gas works, wherryman and warrener. Tenancy often passed from father to son or daughter. Neither Charles Henry Rooke nor Frank Searle lived in any of the properties after their purchase; they rented them out to tenants.

In 1929, Charles Henry Rooke died, and in his will he left 1 and 2 Mash's Row in trust for his grandson, Archer Albert Woods, until he attained the age of 21. The tenants at the time were John Matthews and Walter Johnson. On 29th December 1936, Archer Woods, by then an Able Seaman serving on HMS *Caledon* in Devonport, came of age and inherited his property. Eight months later, he sold Nos 1 & 2 Mash's Row to Harold Matthews, a craftsman builder, who later built both of the extensions on to the houses, and converted a part of the barn into a conservatory.

The six cottages in Mash's Row had, by 1937, passed from the ownership of Frank Searle to Arthur Edward Partridge, an Aylsham butcher, and later sold to Frederick Breese. The interiors of these cottages remained basically unchanged until a combined shower-room and toilet was installed on the ground floor of each one. Numbers 3 and 4 have been converted into one dwelling, and an extension has been built on to the side of the last cottage.

Aylsham residents in the eighteenth and nineteenth centuries were dependent on wells for their water supply and it was often far from pure. The quality of water in the town became a matter of some concern when fourteen cases of typhoid fever were reported in the town in 1904. Clean water was eventually piped in from Norwich City Waterworks as recently as 1938, and even then Mash's Row was not immediately connected to the mains, and for a time a standpipe was provided for the residents' use. The same situation applied to drainage, and Mash's Row was one of the last places in Aylsham to be connected to the mains system in the 1950s. As for lighting, although a gas supply existed in the town from 1850, this never reached Mash's Row, and paraffin lamps continued to be used until electricity was eventually installed in the early 1930s.

Aylsham Town Station at the end of Millgate, near to Mash's Row, was opened in 1883 by the Eastern & Midland Railway which later became the

Midland & Great Northern Railway. Many residents of Aylsham who used this station would cycle to Mash's Row and, for a small fee, leave their bicycles at the blacksmith's shop, and collect them on their return to cycle home. This line was closed down in 1959, the station demolished and the area left as an open space, part of which has been incorporated into the Weavers' Way.

The land on which the houses and cottages of Mash's Row stand is close to the River Bure. Long before William Mash built his properties, this area must have been subject to flooding whenever the river ran high after an excess of rain. There is no documentation on any flooding of this area until the flood in August 1912. It had rained every day for a fortnight, and this was followed on 26th August by 7½ inches of rain, with 6½ inches falling in twelve hours. The river overflowed its banks, and Mash's Row was flooded with the water reaching the first floor windows of the dwellings, and the residents had to be rescued by boat. There was widespread flooding all over the area, which destroyed crops, drowned animals, brought down trees and telegraph poles, and swept away bridges. On either side of the railway at Drabblegate, the meadows were flooded, and a portion of the embankment was washed away leaving the rails suspended over the gap. When the occupants of Mash's Row were eventually able to return, they were faced with the heartbreaking task of cleaning the mud out of their homes. A considerable amount of household goods had been destroyed or damaged by the force of the water sweeping through the buildings. A relief fund was opened by the County and the generous subscriptions enabled money to be distributed to all of those who had suffered loss or damage.

In recent years there have been further floods in Mash's Row, the last one occurring in 1993 after heavy rain. One of the mills higher up the river Bure did not open its flood gates to allow the water to flow through. Consequently, when they were opened, the heavy volume of water broke the banks at Ingworth, flooded meadows in its path, and eventually reached Mash's Row. Following this flood, the River Authority dredged the bed of the river, and cleared the edges of rushes and weeds.

The houses and cottages built by William Mash in Mash's Row are now listed as Grade II buildings. They are a part of Aylsham's heritage, and are protected for the future in a conservation area. So much for the buildings in Mash's Row, now let us look at the man himself, William Mash, who was responsible for their existence, and also look at his family.

The Mash family of Aylsham, 1741–1914

John Mash was born in 1773. His father's first name is unknown. His mother, Elizabeth, was born in 1741, and after the death of her first husband, married a man called Smith. John Mash's wife was also called Elizabeth and was born in 1771. John and Elizabeth had four children – Elizabeth in 1796, followed by Mary Ann in 1798, John Drake in 1799 and William in 1800. The Aylsham Poor Rate books for the years 1814–23 show that John Mash had a farm, and rented glebe land from Rev. N.V. Pitman and Rev. Charles Norris. He also had a malt house.

Mary Ann, the daughter of John and Elizabeth, died on 23rd February 1816, at the age of 18, and is buried in St Michael's churchyard in Aylsham. Six years later, on 11th October 1822, Elizabeth, their eldest daughter, died aged 26 and was buried in St George's Burial Ground, Bloomsbury, London. John Mash died on 13th October 1833 aged 60 years, and was followed on 2nd December by his eldest son, John Drake Mash, aged 34. Both were buried in the same grave as Mary Ann in St Michael's churchyard. John Mash's wife outlived both her husband and children, dying in 1856 in her 85th year, and is interred in the family grave.

William Mash, like his father, was a farmer, and at the age of 23 had his own farm. On 4th May 1831, at the Court of Aylsham Lancaster, Thomas Stoneham, a baker of Aylsham, agreed to pay £500 plus interest for a dwellinghouse owned by William Mash. There is no record of where this property was situated, but it is possibly the first of William Mash's speculative deals to raise money to buy or rent additional land. On 2nd May 1836, William Mash was again before the Court of Aylsham Lancaster, when he presented the will of Sarah Gunner, a spinster of Aylsham. This will dated 17th November 1835 left '*all my messuages, lands, tenements and hereditaments in Aylsham . . . to William Mash of Aylsham, yeoman, his heirs, and assigns for ever*'.

The property that William inherited from Sarah Gunner was situated behind Red Lion Street. Why Sarah Gunner left her property to William is not known, but she could have been a relative. In the same year of 1836, William Mash also rented the Anchor Inn in Aylsham from the brewery company of William Bircham. He appears to have expanded his activities from his small farm in 1823, acquiring further land and property, and these are shown in the Rate Books for the years 1837–41. In 1837, he rented land from W. Wilson in the Walsham Road; three plots from Rev. Philip Hunt, late Vicar of Aylsham; a house and land on the Walsham Road from I. Clearwaller, and he owned land that had lately belonged to Copeman Taylor. He also rented land near Banningham from W. H. Windham, in 1840.

The schedules to Wright's 1839 map of Aylsham gives the following list of William Mash's properties:

No. on plan	*Occupier*	*Description*
209	Jonathan Burrell	Cottages
324	W. Mash	Shed & yard
403	W. Mash	Copeman Taylor's Piece
404	W. Mash	Waste
520	W. Mash	Cascade Piece
529	W. Mash	Cascade Meadow
303	W. Mash	Cottages & gardens

The property 209 refers to the cottages left to William Mash by Sarah Gunner in 1836, and were obviously let at that time to Jonathan Burrell.

324 lay behind the Anchor Inn, and 403 consisted of more than six acres of arable land, while 404 is described as wasteland, and both were situated at Drabblegate.

520 refers to an area of arable land between Drabblegate and Banningham Road.

529 is described as meadow land, situated at the far end of Millgate, near to Drabblegate, bounded on one side by the River Bure and the outlet that flowed to the mill.

303 refers to cottages in Millgate.

All this property and land was estimated at 14 acres, 1 rood, 19 perches, and the rate paid was £5 0*s* 6*d*. The Poor Rate book of 1841 shows that William Mash rented the land of Sexton's Field and Copeman Taylor's Piece from William Wilson, but they were co-owners one year later.

William Mash married Elizabeth Hayne Brett. She was born on 23rd December 1804 at Swanton Abbott, and was the daughter of William Brett and his wife Anne Hayne. William and Elizabeth Hayne Mash had four children who died in infancy and are buried in the grave of their grandparents, John and Elizabeth Mash. On 1st August 1843, a daughter Katherine was born, followed by a son Henry Brett, on 17th March 1845. Both of these children were born in Aylsham and survived to adulthood.

From 1836 to 1846, William Mash is recorded as the innkeeper of the Anchor Inn in Aylsham. In addition to being an innkeeper, he continued to farm the land that he owned or rented. In 1845, he either erected new cottages or renovated those that were already there on a site that he owned in Millgate. These flint and brick cottages are numbers 2,4 and 6 in Millgate, and on the façade of one of them there is a small plaque with the initials W.E.M. and the date 1845.

William Mash died on 24th March 1849 at the early age of 49 years, and is buried in St Michael's churchyard in Aylsham. He left a 45-year-old widow, a daughter Katherine aged six years, and a son, Henry Brett, who was four at the time of his father's death. All the research to find the will of William Mash has so far been unsuccessful, and it may be that he did not make one. His son, Henry Brett Mash, was regarded as his heir, and until he came of age all the properties owned by his father were administered by his mother, Elizabeth Hayne Mash. She continued to farm the land until 1854 and maintained the properties of William Mash, for her son who would inherit them when he came of age.

At a Manor Court on 30th April 1851, Henry Brett Mash was admitted to the property of the Stone House in Millgate, with gardens of an estimated half acre. In the same court he was acknowledged as owning one rood of land formerly called Church Close, which his father had acquired in 1826 on the surrender of Robert Mack and his wife, Mary.

The 1861 census lists Elizabeth Hayne Mash as a house proprietor, living in Millgate with her 16-year-old daughter, Katherine, who was a dressmaker. The Valuation list of properties for Aylsham in 1864 records that Elizabeth was the owner of a house in Millgate, six cottages near the Staithe, eight cottages in Millgate and two near Red Lion Street. The latter two cottages refer to those inherited by William Mash from Sarah Gunner. She also owned six acres of land on the Walsham Road, which were rented by Robert Bartram in 1867, and land and cottages amounting to six acres tenanted by John Nicholls.

The 1871 census refers to Elizabeth as a lodging-house keeper in Millgate, living in the Stone House with Katherine, who was 27 years old and still employed as a dressmaker. By 1874, Henry Brett Mash had inherited all the properties in Millgate and Mash's Row, but what happened to the land that his mother owned in the Walsham Road, the land and cottages rented by John Nicholls and the cottages behind Red Lion Street, remains a mystery as they were not passed on. Elizabeth Hayne Mash died in Aylsham in 1883 at the age of 78.

Henry Brett Mash became an Inspector of Lodging Houses and an Inspector under the Petroleum Act in Downham Market. He was also a Superintendent of Police and the Deputy Chief Constable for Norfolk. He died at Downham Market on 20th March 1912 aged 67 years. In his will, drawn up in 1909, he left £2154 17*s* 11*d* and directed that all his property should be left to his sister Katherine Howlett (née Mash) for her lifetime. After her death, the properties were to be sold by the executors, Walter Bailey, (his brother-in-law) and Frank Searle (a County Solicitor's Clerk) and the monies left in trust for the child or children of his stepson, John Arthur Kidd, for when they attained the age of twenty-one years.

Katherine Howlett, a widow and the sister of Henry Brett Mash, died in 1914, aged 72, at Sidcup in Kent. In her will, Katherine left various small sums of money to friends, and £150 to her cousin Sophia, the wife of William Millett, a blacksmith of Sparham. To John Kidd, the son of her sister-in-law Nancy Mash, she left Henry Brett Mash's presentation clock, her candelabra, and £50 to his wife Kate. After other small bequests, the residue of the estate was divided between her six cousins, Sophia Millet, Emily Calaby, Mary Parker, Annie Maria Howard, Ada Feltham Cord Nutman and Benivento Nutman.

On 28th July 1914, all the properties that had belonged to Henry Brett Mash were auctioned at the Black Boys Hotel, Aylsham. They were sold as five lots:

Lot 1 Six brick and stone cottages with out-houses and gardens in Millgate St. on Gas House Hill.
Lot 2 Three brick and stone cottages with out-houses and gardens in Millgate – adjoining Lot 1.
Lot 3 A dwelling house known as the 'Stone House'.
Lot 4 Two brick and stone messuages with gardens and out buildings, comprising stable and cart shed in Millgate.
Lot 5 Six brick and stone messuages with out-houses and gardens now known as Mash's Row.
For present day reference, these are as follows:

Lot 1 = 2–12 Millgate. [Numbers 8–12 have been converted into two dwellings and No. 10 no longer exists.]
Lot 2 = 14, 16 and 18 Millgate.

Lot 3 = The 'Stone House', 20 Millgate.
Lot 4 = 1 and 2 Mash's Row.
Lot 5 = 3–8 Mash's Row

Henry Brett Mash's brother-in-law, Walter Bailey had died in London in June 1912, and Frank Searle, the remaining trustee, was responsible for the sale. He bought Lot 5 in the auction, and retained this property until it came into the ownership of Arthur Edward Partridge in 1937. Lot 4 was bought by Charles Henry Rooke, Lot 3 the Stone House, was bought by C. H. Meale and then sold to James Flaxman Bond, who later sold it in 1920 to Francis Southgate, a retired Superintendent of Police. The buyers of Lots 1 and 2 are unknown.

The properties and farm lands that William Mash acquired in and around Aylsham have now been dispersed to individual farmers and property owners. This particular line of the Mash family has died out, as neither Henry Brett Mash nor his sister Katherine had any children. All that is left of the family are references in a few old books and documents, the gravestones in St Michael's churchyard and the initials W.E.M. on the houses and cottages in Millgate and Mash's Row.

The Mash family

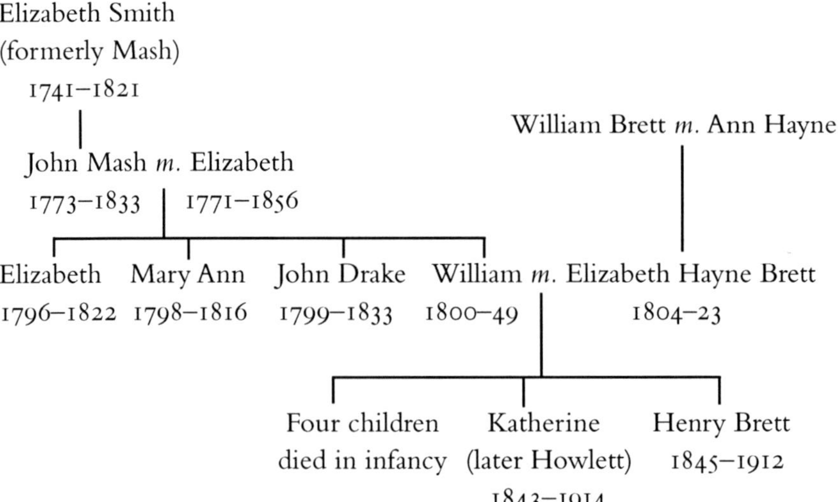

12

Millgate public houses

At one time in the past, Millgate had three public houses and a fourth in Dunkirk, on a road leading from north Millgate to Tuttington. These public houses were the White Horse, Stonemason's Arms, Anchor Inn and Royal Oak. In their time they were patronised by Millgate residents and the wherrymen who sailed along the Navigation Canal delivering cargoes to Aylsham Mill. Other patrons were agricultural workers from nearby farms and the employees of the North Aylsham Railway Station. All four of these public houses have closed, but their history dating from the 1600s until 2001 has been researched and documented.

White Horse

The oldest public house was the White Horse, situated at the beginning of Millgate, just below the junction with New Road and now known as 1 and 1a Millgate. The earliest date found for the White Horse is 1620 and it was probably rebuilt in the 1800s. Although classified as a public house, research has shown that it was often referred to as a small beerhouse. The building was detached and had two floors with a front façade of red brick and small sea coastal flints, a central front door, a single window on the left and a double sized window on the right. Two single windows on the first floor were situated directly above those on the ground floor and a narrow two-storey extension was added to the right of the building at a later date.

A small forecourt adjacent to the road led to the front door and a wide entrance on the left gave access to a rear yard.

From 1620 until the White Horse closed in 1906, a succession of publicans were responsible for running the public house either for private individuals or for the brewery companies who were the owners. One family who administered the running of the White Horse from 1850 until it closed were the Nicholls family, who had a butchery business. During their time at the White Horse, the land behind included stables, sheep pens, a slaughterhouse, outbuildings and a yard. This area has now been built upon with houses and bungalows and is known as Stuart Road.

After the White Horse closed, the owners Steward & Patteson, the Ely and Norwich Brewers, sold it to Arthur Edward Partridge, an Aylsham butcher. He converted part of the building into a butcher's shop by removing the right hand window and installing a large shop window. This shop continued until 1958 when it was sold and the building was converted into two cottages and the forecourt became two separate gardens. The outline of the former shop window can be detected around the right hand window of 1a Millgate as the stones which have been inserted do not match the craftsmanship of the original front.

Stonemason's Arms

Further along on the east side of Millgate was the Stonemason's Arms. In about 1840, the artist Joseph Clover sold a pightle of land and two tenements or cottages to John Freeman, a stonemason. He built a public house on the pightle of land in 1846 and named it the Stonemason's Arms. In addition to being responsible for the public house, he brewed beer and had a successful stonemason's business. When John Freeman died, his two daughters inherited his properties; his daughter Fanny, who had married Richard Chapman, let the Stonemason's Arms to the brewers Messrs Bullard & Co. After the death of Fanny Chapman, her husband inherited the public house, stonemason's yard, one shop and three cottages which were sold after he died in 1926.

John Freeman built his detached public house of red brick, finished with stone corners, a slate roof and a chimney stack at each end. Steps led up to the front door which was centrally placed with a large window on each side, and three smaller windows on the first floor. An entrance on the left led to the back of the building where the underground cellar was located, and at one time this rear area had stables, outbuildings and a brewhouse. The original interior had two rooms on the ground floor for the use of customers and a small room named the Snug, but in the 1950s the two rooms were converted into one and the dividing wall to the snug was removed. Two other rooms made up the ground floor area. The first floor had four rooms; a bathroom and toilet were installed at a later date. Stairs gave access from a landing to two attic rooms and two small storage rooms.

In later years, this public house was only called the Stonemasons, but was referred to by many local residents as the Stonecutters or simply the Cutters. After 1926, various breweries were the owners and the last owner, Pubmaster, sold it by auction in March 2001. After the sale it was converted into a private residence, now known as The Old Stonemasons, 40 Millgate. A sign depicting two stonemasons at work, which had hung on a free standing pole on the forecourt, was removed by the new owner and the forecourt and car park were turned into a garden.

Anchor Inn

At the far end of Millgate on the west side next to the bridge that crosses the River Bure stands Bridge House, formerly the Anchor Inn, which closed in 1961. The first known reference to this property as an inn is in 1793, when it was left by Robert Parmeter the Elder, miller and flour merchant, to his daughter, Ann Lungley, who was the wife of Isaac Lungley, a farmer in Boxford, Suffolk. It was described as 'the Public House in Millgate Street, near the bridge, called the sign of the Anchor; together with three cottages to the same adjoining'. With it went a piece of land (Pond Meadow) and a piece of pasture land lying on the east side of the river opposite Pond Meadow. There is one other reference to the inn, in the same year, in the *Universal British Directory* of 1793, where a John Jennings is recorded as 'victualler'.

Robert Parmeter is known to have bought the property in 1771 from the executors of Thomas Spurrell, miller. It was described then as 'those two messuages adjoining, situate near the bridge in Millgate Street in Aylsham, wherein Hammond Beaton, John Beaton and John Smith now live, and yards and gardens adjoining'. With it went a meadow called Pond Meadow,

The Anchor Inn (now Bridge House) from the bridge over the River Bure

adjoining in part to the yards and gardens of the said messuage (1 acre and 3 roods) in the occupation of Michael Francis, and meadowland on the east side of the river, opposite the last mentioned meadow (½ acre) in the use of Thomas Harvey. The manor court roll goes on to comment that these premises were those to which 'by different description the said Thomas Spurrell was admitted on the surrender of John Webster and his wife, Hannah, in 1753'.

The Websters acquired the property through Hannah's father, Henry Wymarke, who bequeathed it to his two daughters in 1746. When it was surrendered to Thomas Spurrell, the description in the manor court roll is of '16 perches of land with a messuage thereon built, parcel of the Toft Epp; 3 roods of Korrodale otherwise Kurdole, parcel of the said Toft lying next the Great Bridge of Aylsham; ½ acre of land parcel also of the same Toft Epp in Aylsham aforesaid'. We know, therefore, that the property was in existence before 1746, and that it seems to have become a public house between 1771 and 1793, presumably to serve the increased river traffic associated with the Navigation.

In 1830 William Wilson was the innkeeper. In 1833, the property was purchased by Birchams, the Reepham brewers, and in 1836, William Mash, builder and farmer, became the innkeeper and remained so until 1846, three years before his death. James Fitt was the innkeeper between 1850 and 1858. During his time the Aylsham Aquatic Club was formed (on 9th May 1851) and based itself at the Anchor Inn. The first president was Samuel Parmeter.

In the Aylsham directories, between 1858 and 1868, Robert Easton is listed as the landlord. Curiously enough, the 1864 directory refers to the inn as the 'Hope & Anchor'. Still relying on the directories, we have Thomas Wright recorded as landlord between 1868 and 1872. Wright was also the water bailiff during that period. From 1875 to 1888, Thomas Read was landlord, aided by his wife, Mary Ann Read.

In 1878, the Birchams sold the Anchor Inn to Steward & Patteson, the Norwich and Ely brewers. The Statutory Declaration made at that time by William Bircham and Francis Parmeter describes the property as being a public house, with stabling, a skittle ground, a large garden bounded by the river, and three cottages adjoining with gardens behind. 'One of these cottages was many years ago converted into a bakehouse, but is not now used as such, and it is now attached to the public house and used as a Herring Curing House.' Francis Parmeter was the son of Robert Parmeter the Younger, described as 'beer brewer', who lived at Booton Hall.

In the sale notice of 1878 it forms lot 16, and the description includes the following:

> *A carrier's house, just outside the town, on the road from North Walsham, containing large parlour, good Tap, and Bar; stone-paved cellar, kitchen and store room; four bedrooms and two attics; yard in rear, with gates to road, in which is stabling for about twenty horses, and skittle ground; also a good garden, bounded by the river. etc.*

The Herring Curing house obviously continued for some time, as in 1892 James Tight is listed as landlord and also as 'fish curer'.

There must be many gaps in the list of names of successive landlords, but we know from directories that Ernest Clarke was a landlord for a considerable period. He is listed from 1916 at least, right up to 1937 when the county directories ceased to be published, and it is possible he went on for much longer than that. During World War 2, the Anchor Inn became one of

The Anchor Inn in the early 1900s. The cottages on the right have since been demolished.

the favourite watering holes for servicemen in the Royal Canadian Airforce stationed at Oulton. The Canadian, Murray Peden, author of the book *A Thousand Shall Fall* recalls his life at the Oulton base, and he remembers sitting in the bar of the Anchor, where the landlady, Mrs Ena Wilson, let them play through her large collection of Bing Crosby records.

The Anchor Inn, which was owned by Steward & Patteson, closed in 1961 and was sold by auction in 1962. The purchaser, Mr Tom Bishop, has converted it into a private house which was renamed Bridge House. It is a trifle ironic that none of the documents in the 'Bishop bundles', which were loaned to the Aylsham Local History Society for research by Mr Bishop, threw any additional light on the history of his own home, Bridge House, or on its previous existence as the Anchor Inn. The property's connection with the Parmeter family, however, has made it possible to learn something of its history from other sources.

Early 1900s photographs of the Anchor Inn show two doors that led directly from the road into the building and they would have been there before the two messuages were converted into one. Next to the inn were two small thatched cottages which were demolished and replaced with a single-storey building. The 1962 sale catalogue of the Anchor Inn provides information about the building and lists it as being built of red brick with a Dutch gable and tiled roof. Other details described the ground floor as having an entrance with a floor covering of quarry tiles, six rooms, including a kitchen, scullery, larder and a lean-to cellar built on to the rear of the building. The first floor had three bedrooms, a boxroom, bathroom, separate WC and two further bedrooms in the attic.

A wide entrance on the left of the Anchor Inn led to a yard with stables, cartsheds, a harness room and three WCs. In this area there was a former smokehouse used in the late 1800s and early 1900s by two succeeding publicans who smoked herrings brought to the inn from Yarmouth. This smokehouse had fallen into disrepair at the time of the 1962 sale, but has been restored by the present owner. Changes have been made to the former Anchor Inn with the installation of windows that had previously been filled in and a third dormer window has been added between the two original ones in the attic. The front door on the right has been removed and the entrance bricked up, removing all evidence that this building was once two separate messuages.

The Anchor Inn was a detached building set in several acres of ground bordered by the River Bure and patrons of the inn walked along the river bank; Millgate residents were able to have picnics by the river in their leisure time on warm summer days. Many visitors to Aylsham make a point of seeing the historic water mill which can be viewed from the east side of Millgate bridge; few will realise that Bridge House on the west side was once an inn.

Royal Oak

At the end of Millgate there is another bridge crossing an outlet of the former Navigation Canal and further on is a turning to the right known as Dunkirk where another public house was situated. This was the Royal Oak, built in 1843, and although termed a public house, it was sometimes referred to as a beerhouse. It was a small detached building with one bar room entered through a central front door beyond a small forecourt which had wooden rails for the tethering of horses. A ten foot pole on the courtyard displayed the sign of an oak tree in full leaf. An entrance on the left of the building allowed farmers to drive their carts into the back yard and stable their horses. Information obtained about the Royal Oak shows that the ground floor consisted of a bar room, three other rooms and a kitchen. Stairs led to the first floor which had three bedrooms and two other small rooms. Because the building was close to the Navigation Canal and liable to flooding, the cellar was an additional extension built on the right hand side.

The Royal Oak was owned by the brewery company of Youngs, Crawshay & Co. from 1872 until 1938 when it closed and was sold. After the sale, the building was converted into two small cottages and later became one dwelling named the 'Maiden's Bower'. This name can be traced back to 1687 when the site was a meadow called the Maiden's Bower and was in Waterie Lane, which is now known as Dunkirk.

Millgate no longer has any public houses, but the buildings have survived and although their function has changed, they are a part of Millgate's history.

13

The gas works

In the first edition of this book there was no reference at all to the gas works. This was because no member of the original group had chosen to study it. However, the appearance of the gas works was a significant event in the history of Millgate and deserves to be considered in any study of Millgate.

The Aylsham Gas Light and Coke Company Limited was formed in 1849 and the gas works for producing the gas was erected at the top end of Millgate which was subsequently known as Gas House Hill. Some of the building materials were brought up by wherry from Great Yarmouth. The capital for the new enterprise was £1,500 which was raised by the issue of £10 shares. These were snapped up quite readily by the prominent citizens of the town including:

Robert Bartram, builder; William Bell, physician; James Breese, tailor; Rev. James Bulwer; George Elden Burrell, builder; Charles Clements, bookseller; John Wright Clover, farmer; George Copeman, banker; Thomas Copeman, solicitor; John Freeman, stonemason; Lewis Ingate, coachmaker; Samuel Parmeter, merchant; Robert William Parmeter, solicitor; Benjamin Powell, grocer & draper; William Repton, solicitor; William Henry Scott, solicitor; George Soame, miller and merchant; Steward & Patteson & Co; Lady Suffield; Wightman Tooley, farmer; John Warnes, land agent of Bolwick Hall; Rev. Edmund Telfer Yates; and many others.

The list of share allocations issued to the original investors still survives in the town archives and records 41 shareholders in total. Dr Sapwell, in his history of Aylsham, vividly describes the arrangements for the opening of the gas works:

On the evening of 2nd January 1850, the directors attended what might be called a preview when one of them formally charged a retort at the gasworks and they saw the lamp there lighted for the first time. Four days later the gasworks were officially opened amid public festivities worthy of a major national occasion. The church bells were rung at 4 p.m. and the directors and their friends dined at The Black Boys, the room being lighted by gas. There was a distribution to poor people of food paid for by subscription; fireworks in the Market Place at 7 p.m. appear to have attracted the majority of the population, and the day's festivities closed with a ball at The Black Boys attended by over a hundred people.

The streets, most of the public buildings, and many shops and houses were lighted by gas very soon after it became available, and so continued until the arrival of electricity in 1929 provided a more convenient form of lighting. In 1869, 20 years after the opening, it was reported that profits were increasing and the company hoped to make a reduction in price. In White's 1864 directory it was recorded that the streets and most of the houses in the town were lighted by gas at a cost of 7*s* 6*d* per 1000 cubic feet. Other demands on the supply of gas occurred as the town grew. A report by William Henry Scott, Secretary to the Gas Company, illustrates the projected demand that would arise when the new railway station (Aylsham South) opened on 1st January 1880:

This will bring a large amount of additional traffic on the south entrance to the town, and considerable responsibility will be thrown on the inspectors as to such necessary lighting of the road as will prevent accidents arising from what at times will be a crowded traffic of carts, carriages and foot passengers. The whole road into the town is very narrow, and near Mr. Bulwer's barn, and thence to the entrance to the station, particularly so – and at times when the leaves are on the trees in the early part of the Autumn, the road is very dark.

The Railway company will take a large number of lights from the entrance to the station and in the buildings, and for the proper supply of gas the Gas Company will lay a new 3" mains pipe from Red Lion St. to the entrance to the station . . .

The Inspectors are of the opinion that it will require at least four additional lamps to light the road to the station efficiently, it being in their opinion necessary that the last five lamps nearest the station should not be more than about 50 yards apart, and these they recommend the parish to provide; making the best terms they can with the Gas Company for the supply of gas. In the opinion of the Inspectors there is not sufficient width of road to make a separate and distinct footpath for foot passengers, and their responsibility may be considerable unless the road is well lighted . . . The Inspectors would remind the parish that the rating of the railway station will make a considerable addition to the Assessment for the Lighting rate, as the buildings will eventually be large and valuable. They trust that the parish will consent to make the necessary expenditure for lamp posts, lamps etc. which will be about £16–10–0, and they think that the additional supply of gas might be arranged with the Gas Company at about £6 per annum.

Signed

W. HENRY SCOTT

It is interesting to read that 125 years ago the same stretch of the Norwich Road was being considered narrow and dangerous just as it is today! However, the cost of a year's supply of gas for the railway station appears very reasonable.

This is the only photograph of the Aylsham gas works we have discocvered.

World events also affected the smooth development of the gas works. In the company minutes it is recorded that on 25th January 1915 an order from the military authorities was issued, namely that they should darken all street lights, and no street lamp should be lighted from that date until further notice. This order must have been issued following the first zeppelin raid over Norfolk which had taken place six days earlier when a bomb was dropped on Sheringham.

The streets were to remain unlit until the end of November 1918. It has its humorous side. Having ordered all the street lights to be turned off, the military were amongst the first to be involved in traffic accidents in the darkened streets. In October 1917 it is recorded that a lamp post was knocked down and broken near to Mr. Giddings mill, by a wagon belonging to an army driver from the 3rd Company of the County of London Yeomanry. Again in September 1918 a driver in charge of a horse and cart from the HQ Staff of the 320th Brigade did exactly the same thing in Penfold Street. In each case the Military was presented with a bill for £5 10*s* 0*d* for each accident. It took until 1919 before the first bill was settled. The military did not have a monopoly of accidents – in January 1920 the United Automobile Association received a similar bill when one of its buses damaged a lamp on Barnwell's corner.

By not lighting the street lamps, the Gas Company found its expenses reduced, and at the end of 1915 it is recorded that they had sufficient balances in the company's funds and there would be no need to levy a Watching and Lighting rate for that year. When lighting was resumed in 1918, there was a total of 24 lamps in use, and by August 1919 this number had increased to 31.

The streets continued to be lighted by gas until October 1946 when electric lighting, hired from the Norwich Corporation and later the Eastern Electricity Board, was introduced. The original agreement came to an end and the installation was purchased by the Parish Council at a written-down value in March 1957, current still being supplied by the E.E.B. Not many houses are now lighted by gas, but it is still extensively used for cooking and heating. In June 1927, the original company was bought by the British Gas Light Company Ltd., a holding company originally established in 1824, and the Aylsham gas works then became officially its Aylsham sub-station.

In 1937–38 a gas main was laid, concurrently with the water main, along the Norwich–Aylsham road, and the gasometer at Aylsham station kept charged direct from the Norwich gasworks. Local production of gas ceased during 1938. On the nationalisation of the gas industry on 1st April 1949, the Aylsham station became a sub-station of the Eastern Gas Board.

Some of the early officials of the Gas Company can be traced in the Aylsham directories, but the following is probably not a complete list:

Secretary		*Manager*	
W. H. Scott	1854	Henry Kent	1858
Walter H. Mileham	1883		
Henry J. Gidney	1896	Thos Henry Oates	1896
		Edward Green	1904
Robert L. Roe	1912	George Taylor	1912
		Mark Taylor	1916
Andrew Kellard	1929	W. Locke	1929
		W. Robinson	1937

The impact of the arrival of gas lighting in the town must have been considerable. Until then, dusk would have meant the end of most domestic activities until daylight returned the following day. William F. Starling, a prominent local shopkeeper, was born one year after the opening of the gas works. In his memoirs, writing about the 1850s, he describes conditions:

> *Now, the lighting of our houses, yards, etc. The first I remember is sitting with my mother in our living room with two tallow candles and the snuffers and tray . . .*
>
> *We had gas in the shop, but lots of the small shops were lit by candles, but at last gas was general all over the town. We used to get about the yards and stables with a horn and tin lantern, and we had the candle lanterns of glass and tin, also the glass and tin lanterns burning Colza oil, but gradually came down to the paraffin lantern similar to those now used, but very much more primitive.*

(Colza oil was made from cole seed (rape). About 1800 Colza oil lamps came into use which were fitted with a clockwork pump to drive the oil into the wick.)

The arrival of the new gas lighting must have seemed sensational.

The site where the gasometers stood in Millgate is still recognisable. The site was officially decontaminated in 2003–04 by the Gas Board.

Appendix 1

The Millgate documents

The Millgate documents, the so-called 'Bishop Bundles' which were used in the exploration of the history of Millgate and its people belong to Tom Bishop of Bridge House. There are some 17 bundles, and a rough guide to the contents of each bundle is given below:

Bundle 1

a) Two sale notices, 1820. Six lots, 5 in the Cromer Turnpike Road area.
b) Sale notice, 1845. Three lots, including coach and gig works.
c) Sale notice, 1830. Four lots: three of land by the river, the fourth a cottage at Edgefield.
d) Sale notice, 1831. Thirteen lots: 1 and 2 Market Place/Churchyard; 3, 4, 5, 6 and 7 on Millgate; 8, 9 and 10 cottages – Aylsham Vicarage); 10, 11, 12 and 13 on the Turnpike Road.

Bundle 2

The will of James Curties, 1798, and documents relating to legacies, 1803–31.

Bundle 3

a) Documents relating to Thomas Cook's (Bushey) will of 1852(?).
b) Documents relating to land, late Daniels 1906–33.

Bundle 4

a) More documents relating to land as Daniels in Bundle 3.
b) Admission of Thomas Clement Francis to property, formerly of Robert Francis, 1808.
c) Admission of Mrs Anne Bircham to property formerly of Robert Francis, 1808.

(This may be all the same property as bundle 3.)

Bundle 5

Documents relating to the transfer of property from Steward to Fielde on the death of John Steward, 1830.

Bundle 6A

a) Copy of admission of Robert Francis, 1778.
b) Conveyance of a piece of freehold land (Aylsham Wood) from James Mottram to J. B. Aldiss and others, 1901.
c) Copy of admission of Thomas Clement Francis, 1808.
d) Copy of admission of John Fielde, 1823 to land on Ingworth Road.
e) Copy of admission of Mrs and Miss Fielde, 1838.
f) Copy of admission of Ann, wife of Matthias Phillippo, 1846.
g) Copy of surrender by Jonas Warden and wife to John Fielde, 1823.
h) Surrender in exchange to rectify mistake – John Tuck to Ellis Canfer, 1817.

Bundle 6B

a) Copy of admission of Sarah Parmeter (wife of Robert) to a quarter of the holding of Robert Francis, 1808.
b) Acknowledgement of the surrender by Richard Mutten to Robert Parmeter, 1845.
c) Search documents for 15 and 17 Millgate, 1955 and 1957.
d) Estimates for lavatories etc. and plan, 1955.
e) Tithe redemption papers, 1949.
f) Copy of surrender, 1869.
g) Deed of enfranchisement relating to Further 'Doctor's Pightle' and 'North Croft', James Mottram, 1901.
h) Acknowledgement of satisfaction on Richard Mutten's conditional surrender by Jacob Crane, 1845.

i) Copy of absolute surrender by Richard Mutten and wife to Mrs Phillippo, 1845.
j) Letter from solicitor to Mr T. F. Daniels, 1920.

Bundle 7

a) Abstract of title to the estate, late of James Hunt Holley, formerly Hawkins, 1760.
b) Extract from will of George Hunt Holley – discharge for legacies, 1790.
c) Abstract of title of Thomas Rackham and Miss Hannah, 1757.
d) Abstract of title of Mr John Tuck to an estate of Lancaster manor cottages and messuages in Millgate Street, 1831.
e) Copy of admission of Ann Fielde, 1835.
f) Surrender by Matthias Phillippo and Anne his wife to the use of her will, 183?.
g) Account of succession in real property of Ann Elizabeth Aldiss, 5 Ipswich Road, Norwich, upon the death of Matthias Phillippo,1887.
h) James Hunt Holley to Miss Ann Fielde – Act of covenant for production of title deeds, 1831.
i) James Hunt Holley to Mrs John Fielde – copy of absolute surrender, 1831.
j) Copy of admission – Hunt Holley to Miss Fielde, 1835.
k) Copy of absolute surrender – Hunt Holley to Miss Fielde, 1831.
l) Copy of admission of Mrs Ann Eliz. Aldiss (Aylsham Lancaster),1869.
m) Copy of admission of Mrs Ann Eliz. Aldiss (Aylsham Wood), 1869.
n) Agreement of lease for 1 year between J. B. Aldiss and I.Grimes, 187?.
o) Footpath document – alteration (Shepheard family), 1896.
p) Copy of admission of Ann, wife of Matthias Phillippo, 1839.
q) Correspondence with Mr Phillippo about erecting a wall.

Bundle 8A

a) Document relating to the maltings as result of a dispute between Matthias Phillippo and wife and William Belward, 1861.
b) Copy of admission of Mrs Ann Phillippo (Aylsham Wood), 1839.
c) Copy of admission of Mrs Ann Phillippo (Aylsham Lancaster), 1839.
d) Surrender by Matthias Phillippo and Ann his wife to the use of her

will (Aylsham Wood), 1839.

e) Copy of absolute surrender by Mr Bartram and wife to Mrs Phillippo (Aylsham Lancaster), 1839.

f) Agreement between Matthias Phillippo and William and Robert Bartram about Doctor's Pightle, 1860.

g) Receipts of quit rent from Phillippo to Parmeter, 1843.

Bundle 8B

a) Copy of absolute surrender by Mr and Miss Rackham to Mr John Fielde (Aylsham Wood), 1821.

b) Copy of absolute surrender by Mr R. Parmeter to Mr J. Fielde (Aylsham Wood), 1829.

c) Copy of admission of Mr John Fielde (Aylsham Wood), 1831.

d) Copy of admission of Mrs A. Fielde, widow (Aylsham Wood), 1839.

e) Copy of admission of Mr J. Fielde (Aylsham Wood), 1822.

f) Copy of absolute surrender by Mr and Miss Rackham to Mr R. Parmeter (Aylsham Wood), 1821.

g) Abstract of title of Mr and Miss Rackham to an estate in Aylsham ('for Mr Fielde') (Aylsham Wood), 1821.

h) Deed of covenant for the production of deeds, Mr T. Rackham, Mr Copeman to Mr J. Fielde, 1821.

i) Copy of the will of Mr Jonathon Custance, 1742.

Bundle 9

a) Abstract of titles to copyhold estate late Ann Eliz. Aldiss, 1906.

b) Abstract of titles to freehold land late Matthias Phillippo, 1906.

c) Abstract of a title of Mrs and Miss Fielde to an estate in Aylsham, 1778.

d) Abstract of a title of Mr Richard Mutten to an estate in Aylsham copyhold of Lancaster, 1778.

Bundle 10

Map of Millgate basin 1855. Named properties: Kent's Trustees, Phillippo, Parmeter, Bane, Bircham, Wickes, Copeman, Hayne Mash.

Bundle 11

Sale documents for Aylsham mill, 1907 and 1914.

Bundle 12

Relates to No. 46 Millgate and Maiden's Bower, inter alia, Spurrell, Harvey, Bane, Peddar Bane.

Bundle 13

Relates to Power, Drozier and Freeman.

Bundle 14

Refers to Wood and Peterson.

Bundle 15

The Maltings.

Appendix 2

Sources used for this project

The group has drawn on a wide range of material, but the main sources were as follows:

Aylsham Baptist Church bicentenary booklet (1991)

Aylsham Local History Society, *Aylsham Directories, 1793–1937* (Aylsham Local History Society, 2004)

Aylsham Local History Society, *Aylsham in 1821* (Occasional Paper) (1989)

Aylsham Local History Society, *Aylsham in the Seventeenth Century: Documents from the Manor of Aylsham Lancaster* (Poppyland Publishing, 1988)

Aylsham Local History Society, *Journal & Newsletter* (1985–)

Aylsham parish archives (housed in the Town Hall); in particular, records of the Aylsham Navigation, and of the Norwich to Cromer Turnpike.

Francis Blomefield, *An Essay towards a Topographical History of the County of Norfolk,* 2nd ed., 11 vols. (1810)

Census returns for Aylsham 1841–91 in the Norfolk Heritage Centre in the Norfolk and Norwich Millennium Library at the Forum in Norwich.

Owen Chadwick, *Victorian Miniature* (Hodder & Stoughton, 1960)

Rae P. Collins, *A Journey in Ancestry* (Alan Sutton, 1984)

Directories (White, Harrod, Kelly, Pigot etc.) for the nineteenth century

H. M. Doughty, *Friesland Meres and Through the Netherlands: the Voyage of a Family in a Norfolk Wherry* (Jarrold, 1900)

Elizabeth Gale, *Aylsham Inns and Public Houses* (Aylsham Local History Society, 2001)

R. W. Ketton-Cremer, *Norfolk in the Civil War* (Faber, 1969)

R. H. Mason, *The History of Norfolk*, part 5 (1885).

Millgate deeds lent by Mr Tom Bishop (see Appendix 1)

Geoffrey Nobbs, 'Aylsham River in the last century' in Aylsham Local History Society *Journal and Newsletter* 3 (1992), pp. 173–8

Norfolk Ancestor: Journal of the Norfolk & Norwich Genealogical Society (1977–)

Norfolk Record Office (NRO) Aylsham records:

- Aylsham Tithe map schedule 1839 (NRO 303)
- Diocesan Records; wills and inventories
- Manorial records – Aylsham Lancaster, seventeenth to nineteenth centuries
- Aylsham Vicarage records – Aylsham Wood, seventeenth and eighteenth centuries
- North Walsham & Aylsham Primitive Methodist Circuit records (FC 47)
- Norwich Archdeaconry records – wills and inventories
- Papers of Joseph Clover of Colby and of Mary Berry (MC 119)
- Parish records (PD 602)
- Registers of Dissenters' Meeting Houses (DN/DIS/1/2)

Ordnance Survey maps

Riches diectory 1843: included in *Aylsham Directories, 1793–1937* (Aylsham Local History Society, 2004)

John Sapwell, *A History of Aylsham* (Rigby, 1960)

William Frederick Starling, *Memories of Aylsham* (Aylsham Local History Society, 2000)

Wright's map of Aylsham, 1839, and accompanying schedules

Other sources include records of births, deaths and marriages, and microfilmed wills, at the Family Records Centre in London.

Index

PUBLICATIONS OF THE AYLSHAM LOCAL HISTORY SOCIETY

Aylsham in the Seventeenth Century
Documents from the Manor of Aylsham Lancaster, researched by the ALHS.
(Poppyland Publishing, 1988) ISBN 0 946148 32 5

The Poor in Aylsham 1700–1836
Edited by Julian Eve. (Occasional Paper no. 2)
(ALHS, 1995) ISBN 0 9521564 1 5

A Backwards Glance: Events in Aylsham's Past
Edited by Geoffrey Gale.
(ALHS, 1995) ISBN 0 9521564 6 6

A Survey Map of Aylsham
From the original map in the Town Archives. Prepared by James Wright in 1839; maps redrawn by Geoffrey Gale; schedules and indexes prepared by Tom Mollard.
(ALHS, 1995)

Aylsham Regatta
Colour postcard reproduction of an 1850 painting by W. Mileham in the possession of Aylsham Town Council.
(ALHS, 1995)

Aylsham in 1821
Census of the population of the parish of Aylsham, taken by William Morris in May 1821, edited by Tom Mollard. 2nd ed. (Occasional Paper no. 1)
(ALHS, 1997) ISBN 0 9521564 2 3

Six High and Lonely Churches
By Peter Holman. 2nd ed. (Occasional Paper no. 3)
(ALHS, 1998) ISBN 0 9521564 7 4

Memories of Aylsham: the Memoirs of William Frederick Starling, 1851–1937
Edited by Ron Peabody.
(ALHS, 2000) ISBN 0 9521564 3 1

Aylsham Inns and Public Houses: a History
By Elizabeth Gale.
(ALHS, 2001) ISBN 0 9521564 8 2

Aylsham Directories 1793–1937
These 47 directories record the industries, people and families that have taken place in this small market town over a period of 144 years.
(ALHS, 2004) ISBN 0 9521564 4 X

Lightning Source UK Ltd.
Milton Keynes UK
UKOW04f1125010813

214741UK00008B/270/P